Untangling the Web

"Jennifer Schneider and Rob Weiss… have helped many."

—Patrick Carnes, Ph.D., author of
Out of the Shadows: Understanding Sexual Addiction

"A practical and nonjudgmental resource for understanding the challenges of the Web. *Untangling the Web* also offers steps for healing for those who are caught in the Web. I shall recommend this book both to therapists and clients."

—Ralph H. Earle, Ph.D., A.B.P.P., Founder,
Psychological Counseling Services, Ltd., Scottsdale, AZ

"Packed full of non-shaming, clinically sound advice, Schneider and Weiss offer a practical, step-by-step approach to help people break free of compulsive cybersex behavior. *Untangling the Web* is a valuable book for anyone having difficulty with their own Internet use and a tremendous resource for any helping professional."

—M. Deborah Corley, Ph.D., co-author of *Disclosing Secrets* and
Embracing Recovery; Founder of Sante Center for Healing

"*Untangling the Web* is an easily readable book [for] those needing to learn about the benefits of the internet as well as the perilous pitfalls of being ensnared by it…. It ought to be required reading to beginners in recovery."

—Martha Turner, M.D.

Untangling the Web

SEX, PORN, AND FANTASY OBSESSION IN THE INTERNET AGE

Robert Weiss
LCSW, CAS

Jennifer Schneider
MD, PhD

alyson books
NEW YORK

To those struggling with secrets—hiding away from those they might love—we dedicate this book in the hope that they will find their way home.

The descriptions and stories in *Untangling the Web* purposely do not identify individuals. As confidentiality lies at the very center of the psychotherapeutic relationship, we have taken the most exacting measures to preserve the privacy of all real persons. All names are fictitious and all other recognizable features have been changed. Some individuals who appear in the book willingly gave their consent to be anonymously portrayed. In these cases no information has been included that might in any way identify them. Other people and circumstances portrayed in these pages are composite in nature; that is to say, each case represents a great many individuals whose characteristics and experiences have been adapted conceptually, carefully altered in their specifics, and combined to form illustrative viewpoints, characters, and stories. Any resemblance of such composites to any actual persons is entirely coincidental.

Manufactured in the United States of America.
This trade paperback original is published by Alyson Publications, P.O. Box 1253, Old Chelsea Station, New York, New York 10113-1251.
Distribution in the United Kingdom by Turnaround Publisher Services Ltd., Unit 3, Olympia Trading Estate, Coburg Road, Wood Green, London N226TZ England.

First Edition: November 2006

06 07 08 09 **a** 10 9 8 7 6 5 4 3 2 1

ISBN 1-55583-968-1
ISBN-13 978-1-55583-968-0

An application for Library of Congress Cataloguing-in Publication Data has been filed.

Book design by Victor Mingovits.

For Jessica.

Contents

Acknowledgments

The authors wish to thank the following colleagues and friends for their invaluable help with this book: Patrick Carnes, Deborah Corley, David Delmonico, Elizabeth Griffin, Omar Minwalla, Alex Katehakis, John Sealy, Cecilia Quigley, Wendy Maltz, Claudia Black, Jane Nunez, Marnee Feree, Ralph Earle, Reid Finlayson, Linda Hudson, Charlotte Kasl, Dana Putnam, Carol Ross, and Rich Salmon. We also gratefully acknowledge the support of our families, the help of our agent Edite Kroll, and the wonderful people at Alyson Books: Jeff Theis and Shannon Berning. Most of all, this book could not have happened without the many recovering people who put their trust in us and told us, often in great detail, how pornography, cybersex, and sex addiction affected their lives.

Introduction

WHY ANOTHER BOOK about pornography? Erotic images are as old as the hills, and thousands of pornography books and books about pornography have been written. Millions of people view pornography and enjoy doing so. You may be one of them. You may also be one of those people who wonder whether their involvement with pornography is a problem. Perhaps you are in a relationship with someone who enjoys sexual images, who seems to be spending too much time doing so, and who could be—in your opinion—abusing porn. His or her porn use may be causing problems in your relationship, or you may simply be uncomfortable with it. You wonder whether there is something wrong with your partner—or with you—and where to find support and the answers to these questions.

In this book you will learn why pornography use is rapidly expanding, why for some people (and for those who love them) it is a bigger problem than ever, and what you can do about it. You will learn about the role of the computer, the range of sexual activities available on the Internet, and the potential adverse consequences for the user, their partners or spouses, their children, their career, and their safety. This book is for those who are partnered or married and for those who are single; it is for straight and gay people; the religious and those who abstain from faith; for pornography and sex addicts; and for those who may love a sex addict or cybersex abuser and want to understand the problem and how to get help.

We, the authors, have spent many years working with people with sexual problems and see every day the pain, shame, and loss experienced by those lost in addictive sexual behaviors.

We understand the empty family lives and love lives of those left behind when a partner becomes increasingly entangled in the web of pornography on the Internet and sexual escapades in the real world. We also know that these problems can be identified, confronted, and redirected. That is why this book has been written. To those seeking answers and help, read on.

∾

UNTIL VERY RECENTLY, pornographic images were primarily accessed one at a time through print, film, and video. Today, however, by far the most common technology used to access porn is the computer. Internet pornography is a huge business, accessible on millions of Web sites and earning billions of dollars for its purveyors. In 2001, we first published a book called *Cybersex Exposed: Simple Fantasy or Obsession?* about people who become hooked on computer porn. Since that time, computers and the Internet have assumed an ever-larger role in the lives of people worldwide. The Internet has facilitated research and communication, made information in all areas much more widely available and accessible, and provided new kinds of entertainment and support groups. As rapidly developing computer technology has made businesses and governments increasingly dependent on the computer, it has also increased the scope of problems for users who access sexual sites. Living without the computer seems like an unrealistic option for most people. If the computer is causing difficulties, the choice is no longer how can I manage without it, but rather, how can I live safely with it?

Since the publication of our earlier book, cybersex (various forms of sex on the Internet) has basically become understood to be just another form of pornography. In 2001, this was not as apparent, but today one cannot open a newspaper without reading about the latest arrests for online pornography abuses.

The number of people in trouble from their Internet sexual involvement continues to grow, and for some, it is getting more and more difficult to contain their problem. Children and teens are being affected by sexual content on the Internet. They are accessing the Net at a younger age and simultaneously being exposed to adult sexual content. Some become victims of predatory adults, while other young users can fall prey to compulsive cyberporn use even as preteens.

In fact, the cultural changes that we observed through our clinical experience and research in the five years since *Cybersex Exposed* was first published are so significant that we felt they warranted a second fully revised and updated edition with a new title: *Untangling the Web: Sex, Porn, and Fantasy Obsession in the Internet Age*. This new book features the latest information, more personal stories, and tried-and-true advice.

∾

ALTHOUGH THERE ARE many views about whether pornography is wrong or right, harmful or entertaining, and a multitude of moral, ethical, and religious beliefs on the subject, it is not the intent of this book to define these issues. While many think that *something needs to be done* about porn—or Internet porn—it is not the purpose of this work to offer large cultural or political solutions. We, the authors, support every adult in his or her right to engage in whatever type of sexual activity and experience that provides both them and their partners pleasure, satisfaction, and fulfillment provided that their choices are consensual. We do not believe that we or anyone else has the right to judge or discriminate against a person's sexual decisions, provided that those choices do not violate the intrinsic rights and safety of others. We also respect and believe in the rights of children not to be sexually exploited nor exposed to sexually oriented material. Our work is not focused on what is morally or politically correct for any individual or the culture at large. We are not "sex-negative" nor do we promote censorship. Our goal is simply to help those who may have a problem with pornography, and those who love them, find understanding and help.

Pornography abuse or addiction are not of concern to most people, any more than drinking, eating, or gambling are problematic for everyone who drinks alcohol, eats, or gambles. But as long as substances and behaviors can bring people pleasure and distraction, a small percentage of people will abuse those very pleasures, only to find themselves eventually hooked and broken by them. Porn and sexuality are no different. While offering pleasure, healthy intimacy, and distraction to most, they can bring punishment and destruction to the small few who use them addictively. It is to those people and the ones who care about them that this book is addressed.

Untangling the Web identifies the many types of problems that some people have because of their relationship with pornography—online and offline—while offering concrete solutions toward lasting change. The purpose of our work is to inform those whose lives are compromised by their sexual behaviors that these issues can be treated and that help is available should they desire change.

The stories and characters portrayed in this book are based on our actual clinical experience, research, and interactions. We have changed names, combined stories, and highlighted issues both to underscore the issue being examined and to protect the identities of the persons involved. But overall, what is written represents the issues brought before us every day. To those whose lives have become tangled up in a web of lies, self-deception, secrets, and isolation caused by addictive sexual behavior, we offer understanding, hope, and a chance to heal.

In upcoming chapters, we will describe in greater detail what constitutes pornography abuse, how pornography addiction is identified, and what to do about it. We will look at how people can become enmeshed in cybersex and online romantic obsession, at Internet fetish and alternative lifestyle issues, and at the perspective of spouses or partners of pornography abusers and addicts. Parents who have concern over their children's access to pornography and sexual content on the Web will be offered helpful suggestions and advice to deal with this problem. Subsequent chapters will guide those with a porn problem or sexual addiction toward the help they need to heal themselves and their relationships. It's time to untangle the web. . .

Robert Weiss, L.C.S.W., C.A.S.
Jennifer Schneider, M.D.

CHAPTER ONE

Pornography: Fantasy or Obsession?

My husband just admitted to an Internet porn addiction. The admission was the final straw that broke our marriage.

I am a young man who is struggling badly with Internet porn. I need to get this addiction under control because it is hurting my relationship with God and those I love.

I am certain that my fiancée is addicted to online sex and may have even met with other men for encounters. I am totally devastated. She has denied this despite my having found e-mails confirming my fears. I don't know what to do, please help me.

I have accepted that I have a pornography addiction. I am seeking help as it has jeopardized my marriage and my life.

ᔡ

IN THIS CHAPTER we will explain why the Internet is such a powerful outlet for pornography. We will introduce you to the types of activities that are available on the Net, and we will help you understand the difference between recreational and compulsive use of computer porn—use that leads to significant unwanted consequences. If you are a consumer of porn or cybersex, our checklist will help you determine whether your behavior is just fun or is causing you problems. If you are someone who loves a cybersex user, this chapter will help clarify whether your concerns are warranted or not.

THE MEDIUM

PORNOGRAPHY IS BIG business. Taken as a whole, adult and sexually oriented DVD, magazine, book, and online site sales reach into the billions of dollars. While reliable statistics are useful to help examine any issue, exact figures for the adult industry are difficult to determine as the highly political nature of the topic leads seemingly diverse sources to inflate and distort the real numbers. While the porn industry itself encourages the idea that it has billions of viewers to help foster its legitimacy and raise potential advertising revenues, anti-porn activists also generally quote inflated figures in their attempt to point out pervasive problems of pornography. What is crystal clear is that more people than ever before can access and purchase an ever-expanding selection of sexually explicit materials and experiences ranging in content from seemingly benign, traditional pinup-type photos to graphic images of extreme sexual violence and degradation. The computer and the Internet have today become the primary resource for porn and sexual content. Due to its immediate and interactive nature, the online world has produced unique and new forms of sexual content such as "virtual sex" and "online prostitution." However, more traditional forms of pornography such as magazines, films, and DVDs remain as popular as ever.

While many people may frequently enjoy viewing adult magazines or films as a part of pleasuring themselves or someone else, for some people the use of this material becomes obsessive and compulsive. Statistics on sexual addiction suggest that somewhere between 5 and 8 percent of adults have the kind of sexual problem that drives them to use sexual material and behaviors as a means of emotional escape and avoidance.[1] This research, done before the advent of the Internet and online sex, explicitly pointed out that some people with addictive tendencies could become hooked on a relationship with pornography that eventually becomes a detriment to their lives. For these people, the collection and viewing of and masturbation to porn magazines, stories, and video becomes more important than their relationships, work, or self-care. Sometimes subtly hidden, but often not so subtly, their use of sexual material for emotional survival can lead to painful losses and life lessons.

∾

JEFF REVEALS HIS experience:

> I was alone a lot when I was a kid and easily found my way into my dad's porn stash. Looking back, I can see that it was not in my best interest that my dad left his porn around because at 8 and 9 years old I don't think that I was ready to be exposed to anything that explicit, but it was there and I looked at it a lot. And there was a lot! My dad often had stacks of sex magazines in his room and closet, never just one or two. When I started my own porn collection as a teenager I just figured, "like father, like son." It wasn't until I got married and my wife began objecting to all the sexual material I had coming to the house that I even considered that my having collected hundreds of sex magazines and videos might be slightly unusual. In my mind, some people collected cars or watches; this was my collection and I even put certain magazines in plastic sleeves, like collectable comic books. The problem started with my wife's reaction to all of this. Whereas I can be quite reasonable and sympathetic in most of our discussions, when she brought up the porn I got

furious. I didn't want to hear about it. The more she talked about feeling diminished by the images I viewed and that our sex life was affected by my daily masturbation, the angrier I got. How dare she interfere in my private life—one I was not going to change just because I was married. I accused her of being too conservative and prudish and demanded that she let the issue go; with great disappointment in me, she finally did. It wasn't until a few years later, when I came home early from work one day I found my own 7-year-old son curiously watching porn videos I had just the night before downloaded to the computer. I came to realize that not only was there really a problem, but that I was now passing it on to my own child.

∾

STORIES LIKE THIS are frequently told by those with problems related to porn abuse and porn addiction. Some common characteristics of this problem, which we will look at in more detail later, are a family history of early exposure to sexual material or activity; anger and defensiveness when questioned about porn use; lack of empathy at how the porn use might be affecting others; and a belief that "the way I look at porn and sex must be like everyone else" (denial).

While most large urban areas relegate and regulate sexually oriented businesses to the fringes of their commercial and industrial districts, adult bookstores and theaters are as busy as ever, offering coin-operated video porn booths and large screen showings. Rush hour and late evening in any big city is prime time for these outlets to fill up with men stopping off for a quickie by themselves or perhaps with another before going home, or as a part of a night's entertainment. Five minutes or five hours or more can be spent looking at films and images or having anonymous sex tucked away from the rest of the world.

STEVE TELLS HIS story:

> *Even when I got into a relationship, I would stop by the adult bookstores daily, sometimes a couple of times a day. I was going so often that the owners and workers in some of these places started greeting me when I came in, pointing out the newest products and videos they thought I would enjoy. Since I am in sales and most of my work was done from my car and home, it was easy to head out to a day at work but only spend a few hours in the morning actually working and the rest of the day masturbating to porn in a sex shop or adult movie house. I never felt like it was cheating or anything because I was "just looking," no touching, and I figured it was the same as lots of other guys do—there certainly were a lot of other guys there. I never thought of it as "sleazy" or "gross," it's just what I did, like buying groceries or walking the dog; however I never told my spouse, or anyone else for that matter. It was like an exciting secret life that belonged just to me. By the time I finally stopped I estimate I was spending twelve to fifteen hours a week in those kinds of places—and at a dollar a minute to see the films, I was probably spending a hundred dollars or so in any given week. I realize now that I got a lot of my excitement just by driving to the place, planning my time, parking out back, and cruising the booths for the best films. I think the whole process of doing it was as exciting to me as the images themselves. It became an important part of my life and a hard one to give up.*

∽

STEVE'S EXPERIENCE ADDS further dimension to the profile of someone who abuses or is addicted to pornography. His continued involvement at the adult bookstores despite being in a meaningful, intimate relationship, feeling entitled to the sexual activity, justifying that "it's not cheating" even while hiding it from his significant other, and most important, defining the "rush" and "intensity" of the entire experience as the driving force behind it (rather than just the sex itself) are all key elements to having this kind of sexual problem.

THE INTERNET REVOLUTION: NEW OPPORTUNITIES AND CONVENIENCES

THE INTERNET HAS profoundly transformed our culture and our world in ways that can only be compared to the introduction of the telegraph and telephone in the mid- to late nineteenth century. An interactive system connecting personal computers, the Internet was virtually unknown before 1993, when only a few people in laboratories, universities, and the US government utilized it. Statistics[2] tell us that today, only a decade or so since online access first began to be integrated into our culture, approximately 225 million people in North America regularly use the Internet for work, school, or personal recreation—a number that as of this writing reflects nearly 68 percent of the entire U.S. population;137 million people are online on a regular basis![3] You are undoubtedly one of those people and it may even be hard to imagine how you got along before the computer and the Internet came along. The Internet continues to experience phenomenal growth, offering an unending array of opportunities to learn, play and connect with people, and to gather encyclopedic information on nearly any subject or question. It provides rapid, inexpensive communication with people all over the world. If you travel, you are undoubtedly grateful that you now have easier and less expensive options for keeping in touch with your family. Those who travel to the far ends of the globe today have no trouble, even in small towns, finding Internet cafes from which photos and e-mail can be sent out for friends and relatives in the United States to read at their convenience.

In our online world, access to up-to-the-minute information is no longer limited. People with chronic illnesses greet their doctor with computer printouts of the latest treatments for their specific medical problem. Online discussion groups allow free exchange of information and support for thousands of hobbies, medical conditions, and personal concerns. Webcams (cameras) and the easy transfer of digital photographs now allow loved ones to witness important family events in real time from thousands of miles away. Thousands of online chat groups and bulletin boards are geared toward every possible hobby, interest, and pursuit—from '50s automobiles to Zen Buddhist retreats. More people have more access to more information than ever before. And they can find it on their own through their computer, telephone, or PDA (personal digital assistant).

KEEPING UP THE PACE

HAVE YOU EVER watched an old-time classic movie or read a nineteenth-century novel and been disappointed at the molasses-slow pace? Did you know that current television programs and movies now have far shorter and more numerous scenes than those made just few years ago? The rapid scene changes of the music-video world have become our entertainment norm. Inexorably and without being aware of it, we have become accustomed to a much faster pace in many areas of our lives.

The Internet is a logical extension of this accelerating pace. A hundred years ago life was very different. A visit to a relative who lived ten miles away was a major trip. It required an entire weekend to get there, visit, and return. A one-week turnaround time in response to a letter was considered quick. News events in Europe took many days to be publicized in the United States. After April 15, 1912, when the "unsinkable" *Titanic* collided with an iceberg and sank in the Atlantic Ocean, it took days before most people in the United States were aware of this tragedy. Today, news of a commercial plane crash is widely disseminated throughout the world within minutes. A hundred years ago, the first telephones radically altered our expectations of personal communication to a more rapid response time. More recently the popularity of fax machines in the late 1980s resulted in the ability to transfer written documents long-distance within minutes. But even then, people still had to rely on books and libraries for research and bookstores for access to new books and magazines.

The Internet has increased our expectations even further. Why learn at the library when the Internet can provide instant answers to nearly any question from a home computer or mobile laptop? Our culture is increasingly time sensitive, and many people are simply too busy to wait for much of anything. We need information at our fingertips and we want it now. The Internet is there to satisfy our increasing need for quick answers, instant gratification, and immediate action. Not surprisingly, some people who use the Internet to obtain information have also found it to be a fast and easy way to meet their sexual needs and desires.

SEXUAL ADVENTURES THROUGH THE INTERNET

SEX, SEXUALITY, AND sexual expression of every conceivable variety and type have evolved as a dominant area of content and fascination on the Internet. In fact, online access to sexual material and experience has been one of the key financial engines driving the development of the Internet itself. And no wonder—while accurate statistics are often unclear, one 2004 study suggests that in that year there were more than 420 million individual pages of pornography online bringing in an estimated income of 2.5 billion dollars![4] To quote Oprah Winfrey from her show on pornography addiction, "That's billion, with a B!" A study of worldwide Internet use suggested that in 2005 there were more than 72 million visits worldwide to pornographic and/or sexual content Web sites. Understandably, words like "cybersex," "cyberporn," "virtual sex," and "cyber infidelity" have now joined our popular lexicon.

Without the fear of discovery or potential embarrassment of a face-to-face interaction, people are asking about, investigating, and exchanging information about the most intimate details of sexuality and relationships in ways never before possible. For most of these visitors, the Internet provides a fascinating new venue for access to learning about and experiencing sex. For these people, computer sex is but one more way to enjoy life, much like an occasional exotic dessert. The variety and novelty of cybersex may lead some to indulge in it temporarily—even to excess—but most soon return to their usual sexual activities, relegating Internet sexual exploration to an occasional distraction. For some cybersex adventurers, their new online experiences can provide added energy, information, and enthusiasm for sex with self, spouse, or significant other. Others engage the Internet seeking new opportunities for meeting a significant other, dating, or casual sex. When asked, some will affirm that cybersex can be a hot, exciting, and playful distraction, while others see it as a highly engaging way to meet potential dates and partners. However, a significant minority of men and women have found that the ease of access, anonymity, affordability, and interactive technology of the online sexual material have become increasingly problematic. They find themselves hooked on a relationship with online porn and cybersex that has led to reduced productivity, job loss, and relationship problems, as well as health and legal or other concerns.

HOW BAD IS THE ONLINE PROBLEM?

IN THE FIRST decade of the twenty-first century, more and more people are getting hooked on the Net, resulting in significant problems for themselves and their families. The authors have received many letters from men and women who have gotten tangled in the Web and are seeking help.

❧

I have joined a porn site again and have spent the last week e-mailing women for sex. I am online twenty-four hours a day. I have not worked. I hardly sleep. I am useless.

I am concerned about my addiction to pornography. I feel it has kept me from taking the risks needed to be intimate enough to have a real relationship with someone else. I'm 32.

I have lost someone I loved very much due to my cybersex and porn addictions. Please tell me how I can get the help I need.

❧

THESE PROBLEMS CONTINUE to increase. A groundbreaking survey by Dr. Alvin Cooper and associates of 9,265 Internet users found that 8.5 percent were sexually compulsive or addicted.[5] These cybersex users spent at least eleven hours per week in online sexual pursuits. They were considered to be addictive in their cybersex use because they generally denied they had a problem; had made repeated efforts to decrease their online sexual activities; and continued going online despite poor academic or job performance, relationship difficulties, job loss, sexual harassment lawsuits, arrests, failed relationships, or other adverse consequences related to their cybersex use.

Approximately 1 percent of those identified as "cybersex addicts" in a follow-up analysis reported a lengthy history of sexual acting out (compulsive sexual activities) and sexually addictive behaviors such as anonymous sex, sex with prostitutes, and compulsive masturbation, that long preceded their discovery of sex on the Internet. This group of people was having sexual behavior problems even before the Internet came along. For them, the appearance of the Internet simply became another means of accessing a longstanding obsession.

Hank, a 46-year-old married man, began downloading and viewing pornography and erotic stories online from almost the first day he got his computer. Over time this advanced to nightly participation in sexually oriented chat rooms while masturbating to the images and explicit communication that other people would offer him online. Despite having no previous history of adultery, Hank planned and carried out two extramarital sexual encounters with long-term online sexual partners, seeking help only when his wife found out about his behavior and threatened to leave him. Hank writes of the many consequences of his cybersex involvement:

Looking back, I am amazed by the immense amount of time and energy I put into my cybersex activity. It created emotional distance, frustration, and impatience in my relationships with my wife and children and took up work time and office resources. Waiting until my wife went to sleep and then often staying up on the computer until two or three in the morning left me, more often than not, getting only three to six hours of sleep, leaving me exhausted, depressed, and physically unwell. Our marital sex life became practically nonexistent and I watched my wife blame herself for my distancing from her. I spent money we didn't have on pay-per-view porn sites, memberships in online sex sites and the Webcam I used to access and engage in live online sex acts. I even bought gifts for some online "girlfriends" whom I never actually met. Several times I had to cancel my credit cards when I found out that the ones I had used to pay for some of theses online services had been used illegally by others. My teenage son found my porn stash one day on the computer and began "collecting" it for himself. He has caught me on more than one occasion viewing pornography. He knows it is wrong and that I am wrong to be involved with it. My son and I have kept the secret of our online porn use from his mother, my wife. I know it's all so crazy, I hear that when I say it all out loud, but still I have to admit that I think about getting back online all the time.

Triangulation

❧

AND IT ISN'T only men who have these problems. Rosalie is a married 35-year-old systems analyst. Having made it through a rough and impoverished childhood, which she had decided to just "put behind me," she was pleased finally to have a peaceful and stable family of her own. A mother of two children, she felt content with her life. This changed rapidly with her discovery of online sex:

One day at work I accidentally stumbled across a porn site by hitting the wrong key when looking for a business Web site online. Curiosity is why I went back. Within a matter of days, I was visiting porn sites and sexual chat rooms on a daily basis, and within weeks it seems like that was all I did. It literally took control and consumed my life. I went from joining all the free stuff, to accessing anything I could to fuel my interest. I didn't want to go home. I began to lie to my husband about having to work late just so I could continue. I lost my mind in such a short time that I could not function at work or home. It took all I could do to hold up a straight face among my coworkers and family. I became very withdrawn and depressed. My mind became filled with dark and hurtful images, including bestiality. I felt like such a bad person, but I didn't know what to do.

*I guess that cybersex can take some people down a road
they never dreamed they would go. I somehow got sucked
into it and it has been hell to get out.*

THE LURE OF THE NET

HANK AND ROSALIE are examples of people who got
quickly hooked on the net. What is it about computer sex that
can make it so powerful and addicting? Dr. Alvin Cooper, a
cybersex addiction expert, reported that the intensity and
lure of the Internet are powered by "The Triple A Engine,"
that is, the Accessibility, Affordability, and Anonymity of the
Internet.

Accessibility

With more and more people gaining access to the Web
daily, Internet access has grown to hundreds of millions of
people. Moreover, it no longer takes a genius to find your way
around. Computing software, once an engineering mystery,
is now user-friendly with screen icons and helpful prompts
making computer use simple, even for very young children.
Computer-study programming and games have made the
Internet into a educational playground suitable for some
preschoolers; a whole generation is growing up as comfortable
with the computer and Internet access as their parents were
at their age using the telephone. Increasingly today, you can
access the Internet in one form or another not only through
the traditional stationary home and work computer, but from
anywhere in the world via laptop computer, PDA, cell phone,
and portable digital music/video player. Any airport waiting
area, hotel, or coffee shop with a Wi-Fi hotspot offers the
ability to get online and download images and information
from a remote location without the use of connecting wires
or cords. Cell/mobile phones are growing exponentially as a
means of getting online. Today nearly every available cellular

phone system is set up to offer access to the World Wide Web and e-mail at least as an option for the phone owner, which means that the Internet is very, very accessible.

Affordability

In the 1970s, computers were prohibitively expensive, occupied large rooms, and were truly functional only for government and large corporate use. Today, much more powerful computers take up no more than a corner of a desk, are relatively inexpensive, and cost almost nothing to use. An evening spent in a pornographic bookstore or strip club might cost hundreds of dollars, whereas an evening spent on the computer might cost 40 cents unless you are buying images or joining membership sites. Unlimited Internet access is often available without charge. The Internet has made entertainment in general, and sexual entertainment in particular, more affordable than ever before.

Anonymity

As a long-distance medium of communication, the Internet has many possibilities that person-to-person contact does not. It allows the user to try out different roles, to assume any identity or characteristics he or she wishes: A five-foot-four, three-hundred-pound man can present himself in a teen chat room as an 18-year-old high school basketball player or as a 16-year-old girl seeking a pen pal. Most people who visit chat rooms change some facts about themselves, often their age or physical appearance, and even their gender. In a yearlong (2000–2001) survey of more than 9,000 Internet users, 48 percent reported that they changed their age "occasionally" and 23 percent reported they did so "often." Thirty-eight percent of the entire sample reported changing their race while online; 5 percent admitted to claiming occasionally to be the opposite sex, or "gender bending."[6] Many people use false names or "handles" to increase their anonymity.

The Internet by nature is very anonymous. Like most online users, you most likely have a perception of complete privacy in your interactions. Not having to leave home to access sexual material or contact eliminates the possibility of being observed or caught by a neighbor, friend, or coworker somewhere in the midst of a sexual interaction (adult bookstore, massage parlor, public park). Using a computer or portable device, you can access a desired Web site pretty much anywhere—from your own living room or bedroom to a moving car or elevator. People in the past who might have been too uncomfortable or embarrassed to be caught sitting in an "adult theater" or strip club, now savor the same types of activities in the privacy of their home or—all too often—in their office at work, and increasingly in restaurants, bars, coffee houses, or just about anywhere the Internet can be accessed.

The accessibility, affordability, and anonymity of online use make it very attractive, particularly for pornography viewing and sexual intrigue. There are other features that also increase the lure of the Internet for cybersex use.

Interaction

One significant way in which the viewing Internet pornography differs from television, films, and magazines is that the Internet is interactive. No longer does a viewer of sexual content passively purchase a magazine or film and be stuck with what they get; he or she can now sort and reshuffle their images and experiences, changing them at the first feeling of boredom or disinterest. Not only does the online user have control over the endless of sexual words and images, but interactivity also means live interactions between real people in real time. With the Internet, users connect through words (chats) or images (Webcams), actually interacting with the person at the other end. These exchanges can range from simple discussions all the way to live sexual acts being directed through the keyboard while being watched and mutually experienced on screen. Thus Internet technology has the power to hold and keep one's interest far longer than any previous medium for sexual content.

Secrecy

In the past, someone trying to keep hidden his or her sexual or relationship activities had to deal with the problem of physical evidence. Magazines had to be put away somewhere, DVDs and videos taken out of the player, phone calls and sexual liaisons held in secret places. Material accessed on the Internet, on the other hand, leaves less obvious traces. If an unwanted visitor enters the room, the click of a key can immediately close a computer window or cancel a phone or Internet connection, and the user can pretend it never happened. And it is getting increasingly easier to hide and transport large quantities of data. Until recently, pornography had to be stored on the computer itself or bulky disks, making it relatively easy for anyone to find and access that information. Today, with the advent of USB flash drives, the same information can be stored on removable objects the size of a small lighter or pen. These devices can then be plugged into any other computer and the pornography viewed. Space for storing images and data can today be purchased from online vendors and left there, much like the storage units we rent to warehouse records or unused furniture.

Safety

The computer permits the user to engage in real-time online sex with another person—but without the risk of catching a sexually transmitted disease (STD), getting embroiled in an illegal financial exchange (prostitute or massage parlor), or getting arrested (public anonymous sex). Those who tend to be shy or withdrawn can lose their anxious inhibitions behind the more anonymous exchanges available online.

FINDING A COMMUNITY

ON THE INTERNET, users can find a community to validate their sexual interests and behaviors. For some GLBT (gay, lesbian, bisexual, and transgendered) people who may have trouble or feel uncomfortable meeting like-minded others in their community, the computer can provide a very supportive environment and a way of connecting with others with the same interests. The same is true for those with unconventional or culturally frowned-upon lifestyles, such as those interested in cross-dressing or dominance-based sex.

On the Web these people can find other like-minded partners who share and support these behaviors and are willing to engage in them. Thus the constant support and reinforcement of particular sexual behaviors or proclivities can validate these interests in a positive way. It is also easier and safer to find and interact with such people online than in person. Not surprisingly, some Internet users with similar "unconventional" sexual interests have formed "virtual communities" for sexual activities and in support of their sexual interests.

The Internet is unfortunately also a place where people who have deviant or illegal sexual interests such as pedophilia can also find support and validation. Whereas prior to the Internet, many may have flirted in fantasy with various sexual behaviors but were held back from acting them out because of their awareness of potential negative consequences (for example, arrests for child molesting, adverse effects on a primary relationship, or risk to health and life) or because they simply didn't have access to the materials or people with whom they could have this type of sex, on the Internet they can find others who will support and encourage harmful activity. The result can be to normalize subversive sexual behaviors for people who otherwise might never have done them, thereby eliminating the boundary between fantasy and action. The results can be catastrophic for the person's career, freedom, and relationships, and for their potential victims.

SEXUAL ACTIVITIES AVAILABLE ON THE INTERNET

THOSE NOT FAMILIAR with the Internet may be surprised to learn that online sexual activity goes far beyond simple viewing of pornography (cyberporn). Here is a list of sexual activities available online:

- Viewing, downloading, and/or printing porn photos or videos from individuals or commercial sites
- Joining sexual membership communities that serve various interests
- Posting personal sex ads and meeting people for sexual talk and/or sexual activities, to hook up either online or in person
- Chat rooms devoted to meeting people with similar interests through specific Web sites or newsgroups (examples include "Women having affairs," "Spouses up after dark," "She/males tonight")
- Exchanging e-mail and photos with others for the purpose of gathering phone numbers, arranging meetings, or engaging in relating fantasies or sexual talk
- International prostitute, escort, and sexual massage "to hire" sites (some of which actually invites participant to rate the prostitutes they have seen and give recommendations)
- Traditional (print or film) sex-industry products such as magazines and videos
- Simultaneous mutual sexual activity in private chat rooms—writing back and forth
- Live exchange of digital photographs and video—viewing sexual acts in real time using Web cameras

WHERE DOES FUN END AND TROUBLE BEGIN?

EVERY DAY AS more and more people access Internet sexual sites, some find themselves in trouble. Here is a small sample from the news:

- In Salt Lake, Utah, in January 2006, 18-year-old BYU student Daniel George Duke asked a 13-year-old girl if she was a "bad girl" in an Internet chat, then asked her to meet him for sex. Duke showed up at a Salt Lake County park to meet the girl, who turned out to be an undercover officer. Duke was arrested on the spot. (KUTV Salt Lake City)

- Dow Chemical Company fired 50 employees and suspended another 200 for up to four weeks without pay after an e-mail investigation in July 2000 uncovered hard-core pornography and violent subject matter. A spokesman noted that these were not instances about personal uses of the computers and "letters to mom." There was a whole range of abuses from mild pornography to very graphic pornography and seriously violent images. ("Dow Fires 50 Workers over E-mail Abuses," *New York Times*, July 28, 2000)

- Gregory J. Mitchel, 38, of Virginia, was arrested in January 2006 for producing and distributing child pornography through the Internet. He filmed boys engaging in sex acts and received money from Web site subscribers who paid monthly fees for viewing live and recorded videos. Because of a previous conviction on a child pornography charge, Mitchel faced a minimum sentence of twenty-five years in prison. (*New York Times*, January 29, 2006)

- A former US Customs and Border Protection officer, 57 years old, was sentenced to twenty-eight months in prison in May 2006 for having more than 300 images of child pornography on his home computer in Tucson. His sentence is to be followed by lifetime supervision. (*Arizona Daily Star*, May 17, 2006)

WHILE THESE EXAMPLES stand out because they are so public, many people's problematic sexual behaviors never make the news. They simply end up lost in the world of online pornography, "cyber affairs," online sexual chatting—some without obvious consequences, some with extremely negative outcomes. Since the Internet in general, and the Internet's sex sites in particular, can be great sources of pleasure and contain life enhancing information, when are cybersex activities "simply fun," and when do they become a problem and for whom?

Consider David, a divorced 58-year-old man, now having worked for several years to heal from his compulsive sexual patterns. For several years before he found help, while still married, David's sexual acting out took the form of Internet surfing, looking for pornography in newsgroups, eventually downloading thousands of porn images, participating in sexually oriented newsgroups, and engaging in fantasy sex games online:

The many hours I was constantly being on the computer took me away from my business. My sex life has always been one of fantasy. I used to say to myself, "Hey, what's the big deal—I look at porn, masturbate, who's getting harmed. No one." Nothing could have been more untrue! The more energy and interest that went into being on the Net for sex, the less fulfilling any closeness or intimacy with my wife became. No wonder our marriage failed! I also isolated myself from my children and even do not have a healthy relationship with them.

Cybersex problems don't just come from having a computer or access to the Web. I can see now that I had longstanding issues with collecting porn and compulsive masturbation long before ever signing onto the Internet. However, already having a problem with sex, once I got online, I now had access to the largest porn shop in the world—at any time— in any place in what felt like nearly total safety, as no one could "see me" there. It was cheap, with a huge amount just free for the taking, convenient; I could go there twenty-four hours a day and stay as long I wanted. It can and will feed any fantasy, some that I didn't even know I had.

Over time my relationship with pornography became the most important one I had. I protected it, defended it, and pushed others I loved out of the way to remain connected to it. What I now call my sexual addiction problem—in its many forms—has destroyed any real intimacy with the opposite sex and my marriage of twenty-five years, and also made me less available for the conscious parenting of my children. It has caused me to isolate myself from my friends and family. It has helped to further deteriorate an already poor sense of self-esteem and has deepened my depression and at times led to thoughts of suicide. Cybersex has played a real role in bringing me the most depraved thoughts and images that one could imagine. This is truly insanity for me.

∽

WHILE DAVID CAME to realize late in his cybersex addiction that he had a pornography problem, it can be helpful to review your own online activities to see if you have might have sexual issues to work through. We suggest you take the following quiz to find out if you or a loved one has crossed from casual use to a problem.

∾

TANGLED IN THE WEB?

WHEN TAKING THE test, circle yes or no next to each question.

1. Do you find yourself spending increasing amounts of time online looking at porn or engaged in sexual or romantic intrigue? Yes/No
2. Do you become involved in multiple romantic or sexual affairs online at the same time? Yes/No
3. Being truly honest with yourself, do you think pornography use or online sexual activity violates your marital and spousal commitments? Yes/No
4. Have you been unable to cut back on the frequency of your off- or online sexual involvement despite a thought or desire that you should do so? Yes/No
5. Have you been unable to "stay away" from sexual materials, sites, or interactions that have made you uncomfortable or worried about yourself when you previously viewed them? Yes/No
6. Does your pornography use interfere with home life, work, or school (such as making you tired or late because of the previous night's use, or going to sex sites while at work)? Yes/No
7. Does your pornography use intrude on relationships that are important to you (for example, do you minimize a partner's feelings about your porn use, or have you experienced a decrease in your intimate sexual life)? Yes/No

8. Do you collect pornography, keeping hundreds of magazines or videos or images stored in your computer or elsewhere? Yes/No

9. Do you engage in fantasy acts online or view other porn depicting illegal or violating sexual acts, such as rape, bestiality or child porn? Yes/No

10. Has the time you spend interacting with friends, family, and loved ones decreased because of your porn use or fantasy involvement? Yes/No

11. Do you lie or keep secrets about the amount of time you spend interacting with porn, the type of porn you view, or the types of activities you engage in online? Yes/No

12. Do you have sex—either in fantasy online, or in person—with someone other than your spouse or partner? Yes/No

13. Are you hearing complaints and concern from family or friends about the amount of time you spend online using porn or the type of porn you use? Yes/No

14. Do you become irritable, angry, or extremely ashamed when asked to give up or reduce porn involvement to engage with partners, family, or friends? Yes/No

15. Has the primary focus of your sexual or romantic life become increasingly related to images found in magazines, videos, or computer/Internet activity? Yes/No

~

THESE QUESTIONS WERE evolved by listening to and working with hundreds of people who found they had real problems with all forms of pornography—online and off. If you or someone you care about is excessively involved in any one of these areas, or has had problematic consequences as a result of any one of these, it can be a clear sign of a concern that needs to be addressed.

Involvement with illegal online sexual activity (question 9) is *always* a problem and should be brought up with a confidential professional counselor who is skilled with these issues (see Resources at the end of the book to find such a professional).

In general, people who said yes to one to three of the symptoms should openly discuss their concerns with a caring friend or family member. More than three positive answers indicate the need to consider more professional support or counseling. If taking the self-test leaves you feeling uneasy or anxious about your sexual behavior or history, that too is an important sign of the need to reach out for support and direction.

∾

THE NEXT TWO chapters will describe in greater detail the differences between a pleasure seeker and a sex addict, and will point you in the direction of help.

CHAPTER TWO

Pleasure Seeker or Porn Addict?

WHY DO SOME people get hooked on pleasurable activities while others seem to have no problem stopping their fun whenever they wish? How can pursuing pleasure actually hook someone to the point of ignoring the things that matter? This chapter will answer these questions for you.

∾

WHO CAN SAY YES?

WHO DOESN'T FIND the gleaming dessert tray brought out at the end of a good restaurant meal irresistible? Even if you've had enough to eat, seeing all that pastry, sugar, and chocolate is bound to produce some longing and interest. When faced with potentially pleasurable and stimulating activities, whether the pursuit of sex, spending, gambling, or that amazing dessert, everyone experiences temporary chemical changes in the brain that ignite differing degrees of interest and excitement.

When an object of desire comes within reach of a brain, it releases a flood of neurochemicals such as dopamine, serotonin, adrenaline, and endorphins. which are the brain's own mood-altering and pain-avoiding substances. It is that rapid alteration of brain chemistry, initiated either through fantasy or our five senses or both, that leaves us feeling excited and wanting to go forward toward what we see, smell, hear, and desire. We don't even have to actually engage with the activity itself to get excited; a mere lingering thought about a highly desirable experience begins this biologically based arousal process.

Though everyone can be tempted by a potentially pleasurable activity, we each have differing degrees of self-control that help us decide whether to move toward something exciting or stay away from it. In other words, we are able to think before taking action, using our past experiences as a guide. For healthy people, impulsive desires are filtered by intellect, which helps us to consider at least some of the potential outcomes before acting. People with good impulse control have the objectivity to decide whether seeking a pleasurable experience has risks and if so, if the risks are worth the possible negative consequences. In the area of sex they may ask themselves, "Is having this flirtation or looking at these porn images going to affect my relationship?" Someone starting a diet may consider, before diving in, "Is devouring that food going to make me feel ashamed later or work against my goal of losing weight?"

The ability to stop and consider the outcome, *before taking action*, is a key measure of emotional health. However, even a healthy person's ability to "just say no" and control an impulse can be compromised at times, depending on the how strong their desire is and what their level of emotional stress. When we get a raise or have a newborn, we may disregard some of our usual cautions in celebration. But typically, issues such as ongoing personal crises, lack of sleep, emotional losses, and financial concerns are the reasons people cite to explain why they may have been more impulsive than usual. The more anxious, worried, and stressed we are, the less likely it is that we will make the best decisions. People who generally have trouble tolerating their emotions—those who are quick to anger, impatient, and impulsive by nature—have a harder time not reaching for immediate gratification without careful thought.

WHO CAN'T SAY NO?

CERTAIN PEOPLE HAVE a hard time resisting impulses, don't seem to learn from their mistakes, and find themselves increasingly saying yes when they should most definitely say no. Some who struggle with obvious shyness, self-doubt, and social difficulties will compulsively seek out stimulating and distracting experiences as a substitute for the comfort of human intimacy that they find difficult to achieve. At the other end of the spectrum there are other highly impulsive people, perhaps outwardly appearing quite extroverted, even intimidating, who often have similar inward struggles, deep self-doubt, and fluctuating self-esteem, combined with a longing for intimacy but difficulty allowing themselves to be vulnerable enough to become truly intimate with anyone. These people may also struggle with the use of substances and behaviors to escape and avoid pain. As they are generally socially adept, they may get into romantic or marital relationships, which on some level they find unsatisfying because they are unable to be allow themselves to be vulnerable. No vulnerability, of course, translates into no intimacy. Their approach to life is to try to have their cake and eat it too, blaming spouses, families, coworkers, in fact anyone but themselves, for their own unhappiness and unhealthy choices. Because they consistently, impulsively, and unempathically put their own needs above others', these people appear quite self-absorbed or narcissistic. They are likely repeating unhealthy lessons of emotional survival that they learned growing up.

Both these types of people frequently have experienced overtly traumatic or covertly neglectful childhoods and, not surprisingly, many also have close family members with addictive or emotional disorders. Lacking the genuine intimate nurturing every child needs, they learned early in life to cope by using excessive distraction and fantasy. These patterns often left them bereft of the complete skill set required to have their emotional needs met or even of full knowledge of what they need from others, but proficient at using immediate gratification as a means of emotional stability and stress release. Rather than making consistently healthy choices for themselves and their families, people with deep emotional wounds are more likely *to react* than think through their actions. They are also likely to be impulsive, seeking to feel better now while dismissing and denying potential long-term consequences, or compulsive, repeatedly engaging patterns of problem behaviors whose primary purpose is to reduce anxiety. They diligently hide their mistakes, working to look good on the outside, rather than being honest and taking emotional risks with those close to them. For these people, certain triggering situations—such as an extended period of time spent alone, a frequent travel schedule or a weekend with no structure—produce uncomfortable feelings that move them toward stimulating and distracting activities to avoid uncomfortable emotions. If the distraction they use is both effective in making them feel immediately better, however temporarily, and *pleasurable* to them, they understandably might return to it over and over again.

A healthier person might say, "No, thanks, I can see where this is heading and I don't want to go there" or "Once was enough, no need to do that over and over," as have many of us do who have used substances or behaviors in a way that threatened a negative outcome. Narcissistically wounded people, on the other hand, who already feel isolated and unworthy, can easily get hooked on the intensity and variety of compulsive spending, gambling, porn use, or the pursuit of Internet sex as a means of feeling validated and connected. In time, they get hooked on repeatedly losing themselves in the intensely arousing feelings produced by these distractions, some even to the point of becoming addicted to them.

TYPES OF PORNOGRAPHY USERS

SCIENTIFIC STUDIES OF cybersex users offer another way of understanding the mindset of all pornography users, which can range from the occasional enthusiast to the sexually addicted one.[7] These definitions, initially created to describe cybersex and cyberporn users, are organized into three types, along with their chief characteristics. Do you recognize yourself or a loved one?

The Casual User

These are people who find using pornography interesting or fun, and get involved for short periods of time but not to extremes. Ultimately they find it a playful distraction, an occasional form of escape or relaxation, but not a meaningful one. The following is often true of this type of usage:

- Curiosity, novelty, education, or entertainment most often drive the activity.
- Frequency of activity may be driven by life stage events, such as more frequent use in late adolescence or when out of a relationship.
- Viewing is intermittent and occasional.
- Interest in porn is not sustained over time because of lack of face-to-face interaction, the repetitive nature of the two-dimensional images, and the unreality of the activity.

The Pleasure Seeker

PEOPLE BECOME VULNERABLE to addictive distractions because of extreme ongoing life stress or longer term personality problems that leave them less connected to healthier ways of coping. They may intensely use pornography or cybersex for periods of time as a distraction from their problems, sometimes to the point of having occasional negative consequences. While they may have addictive periods of porn use, they will generally respond to adverse external consequences or the bad feelings produced within themselves by adjusting or stopping their behaviors.

Characteristics of at-risk users often include:

- Has a previous history of addictive behavior problems or substance abuse
- Is quick to feel criticized or judged and react—takes things personally
- Has difficulty tolerating strong emotions—tends to act out with rage or sarcasm, by putting down others, and by isolating themselves
- Keeps secrets; is willing to sacrifice intimacy for "looking good," "being right" or "being liked"
- Uses sexual stimulation as a means of achieving distraction from stress or extremes of mood
- Is more self-focused, "narcissistic"; has difficulty relating to or understanding others' frustrations with them; often doesn't see "their part" in a conflict

UNDERSTANDING THE "AT-RISK" PLEASURE SEEKER

Pleasure seekers thrive on novelty and intensity and as such are often eager for the excitement and emotional escape of a new romantic relationship or sexual thrill. This makes them prime candidates for cybersex intrigue, impulsive porn use, collecting porn, and affairs. Though outwardly some may exude confidence, these people have underlying poor self-esteem and difficulty maintaining a consistent, positive sense of themselves, and tend to need consistent attention and validation to bolster their fluctuating self-esteem. Pleasure-seeking men and women are likely to use sexual images and experiences in an attempt to fill the emptiness they feel inside, while at the same time dismissing any problems this might be creating in their close relationships.

While not necessarily addicted or even compulsive about their porn use, pleasure seekers are likely to show similar traits to sex addicts such as hiding their use of pornography; hiding the extent of their use; denying that their use is a problem (even though it may upset a partner or spouse); using the personal ads or the Internet for frequent anonymous or casual sexual encounters (that cause harm to their health, relationships and outside activities); and being more attracted to the perceived safety, intensity, and anonymity of porn and cybersex than to the slower development of more intimate connections. *What differentiates this type of person from a sex addict is that pleasure seekers can stop their sexual behaviors on their own; sex addicts cannot do so without outside intervention and support.*

The Sex Addict

These users are people who become hooked on porn use and cybersex activity regardless of the consequences. They feel driven to engage in the image-driven romantic or sexual activity to the detriment of their personal lives. They are unable, on their own, to stop the addictive behavior patterns and often have previous histories of sexual problems and/or other addictions including substance abuse. Characteristics of sexually addicted users include:

- History of childhood abuse, trauma, or neglect (which they might not accept emotionally, acknowledge, or understand)
- History of addictions in the family
- History of intimacy problems and relationship concerns; they have broken commitments, hurt others, left for no apparent reason, or didn't see relationships through

- Leaving relationships when the initial excitement of a new person or new body has worn off
- Previously established pattern of using drugs, alcohol, food or other compulsive behaviors (including work) as a means of coping with stress or difficult feelings
- Possible history of anxiety, depression, or other emotional challenges
- Social or emotional isolation
- Use of porn and masturbation to replace personal communication and support
- Ability to live a double life—keeping significant information from family and loved ones

UNDERSTANDING THE SEX ADDICT

People who become addicted to using the intensity of multiple sexual contacts, objectifying body parts, and compulsive use of porn for emotional distraction and comfort are much like drug addicts and alcoholics, but instead of using something obtained externally (heroin, nicotine, cocaine, alcohol) to relax or escape, these people have learned to exploit their own natural pleasure-producing processes (neurochemistry) by means of their fantasies and actions. Over time their life priorities shift from work, family, and friends to the pursuit and engagement of sexual content and behavior. Everything else becomes secondary. The neurochemical stimulation provided them by looking at porn for hours, cruising up and down boulevards for prostitutes, or trying to seduce yet another person becomes the drug they work to obtain and protect.

Without outside intervention, most addicts' patterns of behavior tend to escalate over time rather than decrease. Sex addicts continue to act out their compulsive sexual behaviors despite the fact that their actions often leave them feeling bad about themselves and/or cause damaging consequences to those they care about. Some may attempt to stop on their own by switching from one sexual behavior to another. For example, they may move from compulsive porn use to going to strip clubs. Unfortunately, switching types of sexual activity does not solve their long-term problem. This way of thinking is like the alcoholic who, having too many problems when drinking vodka, switches to wine. He is still drinking. He has not stopped, but merely has found a different way of getting the same high. Those who are able to stop their sexual acting out entirely in all its forms and do so on their own are likely not addicted.

Even before sitting down to search and load online porn or seek potential sex partners, sex addicts are already in a sense high. Even before viewing porn or chatting someone up online, they are already emotionally aroused and distracted. Not unlike the dog that begins to salivate upon just seeing a treat, sex addicts are triggered by association, sexual fantasy, and ultimately, behavior, into an emotional state that renders them relatively powerless to make better choices or to consider how their behaviors affect others in the long term. People in treatment for various addictions often call this state "the trance" or "being in the bubble." Hours can go by while they remain paralyzed in their repetitive arousal patterns. This is the same type of emotional state that the compulsive gambler feels when sitting at a craps table, his children's college fund stacked in chips in front of him.

Locked into fantasy and sexual obsession while spending hours online, the cybersex addict's emotionally charged neuro-chemical high is maintained or increased by the ongoing chatting, searching, and downloading of sexual images and experiences. Every new picture, chat, and possibility sends messages to his brain to release more dopamine, adrenaline, serotonin, and endorphins, helping maintain the desired level of distraction and arousal. Like the addicted gambler waiting with bated breath for the next card to be dealt, the sex addict keeps himself in a constant state of physical anxiety and arousal through all this searching and interaction.

This obsessive behavior is not necessarily what we might typically think of when we think of someone being sexual, even though the images or experiences being viewed are of a sexual nature. For example, a sex addict viewing cyberporn can spend hours looking and feeling intense emotional arousal without ever actually becoming physically aroused or having an orgasm. This activity keeps him completely distracted and not thinking of other stressful priorities, relationships, or experiences. If his spouse confronted the issue by questioning, "What about me and our relationship? Didn't you think about how your looking at the porn every night was affecting us?" the reality for the cybersex addict is that he is so totally focused on the intensity of the immediate moment that he literally doesn't think about anything else. Porn addicts can sit in front of their images or computers for hours and hours, even saying to themselves, "I'll stop in ten minutes, I'll stop for dinner, I'll stop to put the kids to bed." Meanwhile dinner gets cold and frustrated loved ones give up waiting and go to bed on their own while he remains online, oblivious to all except the next set of words or images.

Although the final outcome of sexual acting out for some may be an orgasm, for most sex addicts in general the goal of all the looking, cruising, contacting, and downloading is not necessarily orgasm because once orgasm occurs, the hunt is over and reality floods in. At this point, they are reminded of the late hour, promises made and broken, or yet another night of not enough sleep. Herein lies another difference between someone simply seeking sexual arousal through images online and what the pornography addict is looking for: While both may be emotionally and sexually aroused by the images and experiences they are having, the non–sex addict is usually more focused on moving toward an actual sexual act (with herself or another) whereas the sex addict tends to spend significantly longer periods of time looking, searching, and getting lost in the distraction of these activities than in actually having sex.

CHARACTERISTICS OF ADDICTION

All addictions—whether to alcohol or drugs (substances), gambling or online sex (behaviors)—are characterized by three elements that must be present in order to define the problem as an addiction:

1. *Loss of control over the activity* The behavior has become compulsive and the person has lost the ability to stop when he or she wishes, although they may not admit this to themselves or others. They may have tried to stop but over time, cannot do so.
2. *Continuation despite negative consequences* These may include relationship problems, job loss, health or legal concerns.
3. *Preoccupation or obsession* The addict spends large, often increasing amounts of time thinking about, planning, or actually doing the behavior to the detriment of relationships, family life, or work.

∿

WHEN THESE THREE criteria are met, a person can be said to be truly addicted to that activity. Another typical characteristic of addiction is *tolerance*, meaning it takes more and more of the activity to get the same effect. Alcoholics often find themselves drinking more liquor to feel the same euphoria that a small amount initially induced. Pathological gamblers usually bet larger and larger amounts of money more often. Those addicted to online sex often find themselves spending more and more time engaged in cybersex activity and/or find themselves seeking out increasingly more arousing, and sometimes disturbing, images and experiences which offer a more intense experience.

It is typical for sex addicts to become irritable, even outright angry if asked to look objectively at their sexual behaviors or challenged to stop them. They tend to be highly defensive, especially if they have been keeping secrets, and blame those asking the questions for being "intrusive," "prudish," "nagging" or worse. They are rarely able to see or consider how their sexual activity is affecting others, even those close to them. For the sex addict, the relationship to pornography, and unimpeded access to that relationship, is far more important than someone else's feelings or opinions. Those who do choose to stop often find themselves struggling with unexpected feelings of restlessness and anxiety that their porn use had helped to mask.

WHY ME?

If you are addicted to substances and behaviors, then you are likely someone who has difficultly knowing and managing your emotions and reactions. For you irritability, anxiety, stress, embarrassment—even joy—are at times overwhelming, leaving you wanting to escape. The effect that drugs, alcohol, and intensity-based behaviors (such as sexual acting out, gambling, or even self-mutilation) provide is the means for you to tolerate and get through emotional challenge and discomfort. The classic example of the shy person who becomes the life of the party after a few drinks demonstrates clearly how substances allow drug addicts and alcoholics to manage circumstances that they might otherwise find difficult. Addictive behaviors provide a similar coping function for those who do not innately manage and tolerate their own moods and feelings. If you are an addict, abusing or depending upon substances and/or behaviors becomes a logical way for you to manage emotional discomfort, no matter how crazy your substance abuse or addictive behavior may look to those around you. This maladaptive form of emotional survival can be replaced only with proper redirection, support, and the introduction of new skills.

TYPES OF ADDICTIVE SEXUAL BEHAVIORS

In his groundbreaking book *Out of the Shadows,* Dr. Patrick Carnes categorized problematic sexual behaviors into three levels, based on the way society views them legally and ethically. These are:

LEVEL ONE According to Carnes, Level One sexual behaviors have the potential to become addictive but are generally acceptable to current society, though some of them do have the potential to cause emotional harm. They are neither illegal, nor do they involve sexual abuse of others. Level One behaviors tend to be integrated into people's lives, causing problems only if they become excessive or unmanageable. Most people who engage in these kinds of sexual activities enjoy them and are not troubled by the outcome or results. These include:

- Masturbation
- Affairs
- Straight or gay sexual relations with single or multiple partners
- Pornography use and collection, with or without masturbation
- Cybersex with or without meeting up with someone
- Phone sex
- Anonymous sex
- Legal forms of prostitution

LEVEL TWO Level Two sexual behaviors are considered to be nuisance behaviors or crimes, therefore falling out of the boundaries of acceptable behaviors. They often include more deviant sexual activities that have mild but nonetheless serious legal consequences or can potentially violate others. Most people arrested for these activities have a long history of such behaviors, sometimes with previous arrests. The sex addict may occasionally seek a sexual experience for the increased thrill offered by its inherent danger and illegality, but the addict may end up hooked on the behavior, taking increasing risks. These people need some kind of sexual disorders treatment. Their behaviors include:

- Exhibitionism
- Voyeurism, either online with Webcams or live
- Illegal prostitution—providing and procuring
- Public sex (in beaches, bathrooms, parks, and so on)
- Obscene phone calls
- *Frotteurism* (touching another person without permission)
- Stalking, following, or otherwise harassing another person

LEVEL THREE Level Three sexual behaviors involve more significant sexual violation to others and are serious crimes. These include:

- Rape
- Child molestation
- Obtaining and viewing child pornography
- Obtaining and viewing rape, bestiality and/or snuff pornography (photos or online)
- Sexual abuse of older or dependent persons
- Incest
- Sexual violation of dependent persons through the breaking of professional boundaries (doctors, clergy,

police officers, and others who abuse positions of power in order to manipulate others for sex—often not even seeing the power differential as a part of the equation)

∾

EXTENSIVE PORNOGRAPHY USE can encompass behaviors found in each of Carnes's three levels. Viewing Internet pornography and engaging in real-time cybersex with anonymous sexual partners are Level One behaviors. The illicit videotaping of nude athletes in locker rooms and surreptitious videotaping up women's dresses while standing in line behind them ("upskirting")—and transmitting such tapes on the Internet—are examples of Level Two behaviors. Soliciting child pornography online or seeking children for sex through the Internet are Level Three behaviors.

SEX ADDICTION: A PROBLEM FOR MEN *AND* WOMEN

ALTHOUGH MANY ASSUME that addictive sex is primarily a men's problem, approximately 25 percent of the members of 12-step recovery programs for sex addiction are women. Although certainly some women share similar behaviors to men, women's sex addiction in general tends to follow somewhat different patterns from those of men. Because men tend to be more visually focused, they naturally move toward pornographic images as a primary source of stimulation. Women, however, tend to be more relationship focused and therefore are more likely to get into fantasy relationships offline through personal ads and the like and online through chat rooms or sexual dating sites. Whereas men tend to be more voyeuristic, seeking to view nudity and titillating images, women tend to be more exhibitionistic, showing or selling their bodies through

A FEW WORDS ABOUT SEXUAL OFFENDING

Sex addicts are men and women who engage compulsively in one or more sexual behavior, continue these behaviors despite significant negative consequences, and spend a great deal of time thinking about, planning, and engaging in sexual activity. Over time, sex becomes the primary focus of their lives. A *sex offender* may have similar symptoms, but sex offenders differ in that they engage in sexual activities that violate the rights of others, violate the law, or both.

Sex addiction may take away a person's health, self-esteem, marriage, or job, and may personally offend many people, but seeking or having a lot of indiscriminate sex is not sex offending. While many spouses or partners of sex addicts worry that their children or families might be at sexual risk having a sex addict in the house, the reality is that *most sex addicts are not sex offenders.* However, those who seek out images of children or teenagers on the Internet risk having their homes and workplaces raided and their computers or PDAs taken, and being arrested and imprisoned for breaking the law.

If you are looking online for any form of sexually arousing images related to children, including nude "nonsexual" photos, or if you are seeking in any way to meet a minor for sex through the Internet, you will very likely be discovered and arrested. Although the Internet has made accessing such images quite easy, it has also upped the ante for law enforcement officials who are constantly monitoring those they find seeking out such images and experiences.

still photographs and Web cameras. Female sex addicts are less likely to take part in anonymous sexual encounters without at least the fantasy that some kind of special relationship might develop.

Recent research has compared the way women and men use the Internet for sex. In a survey of more than 9,000 Internet users, 14 percent of the entire group were women. However, among those who identified themselves as addicted to cybersex, women constituted 21 percent.[8] In other words, while in general most people seeking sexual stimulation online are male, women are overrepresented among those who indicated that they might have a problem with it. One hypothesis is that women who use the Internet are more at risk of developing sexual compulsions. Another possibility, however, is that women may be less likely than men to deny that they may have a problem, since it is less acceptable for a female in our society to be "driven by sex," use the computer for sexual pursuits, or even look at pornography.

Women's sexual activities online were also found to differ from those of men. Most women are not interested in pornographic images; they tend to prefer chat rooms, where they can connect with a person, and are less likely to use the Web in the specific pursuit of sex itself. Men have the opposite pattern—they prefer porn and adult sites, using chat rooms as their second choice for engaging in sexual activities. This supports women's preference for sex within the context of a relationship, whereas men are more comfortable with anonymous or objectified sex.

Some women do fall into patterns of sexual behaviors that are both intense and self-destructive. Consider Joyce's story. For many years, Joyce, a 34-year-old married accountant and mother of three children, had been an avid consumer of television soap operas and romance novels. These stories would transport her from her mundane existence to a romantic, exciting world of endless bliss in exotic locations.

Though she had not had an affair, she frequently masturbated to fantasies related to coworkers, family friends, and
the fantasy characters in her television shows. When Joyce's
husband Roy, bought a computer for their home, she initially
used it to maintain the household bills while using e-mail to
contact family and friends.

While scanning the Internet one day, Joyce entered the world
of Internet chat rooms, quickly finding herself spellbound by
the exciting men and personal conversations she encountered
there. Within weeks, Joyce was staying up long after Roy was
asleep, chatting with other "marrieds" about their lives and
personal situations. Conversations in open chat rooms led to
regular online "meetings" with specific men with whom she felt
particularly comfortable.

Over several weeks these interactions became increasingly
more intimate, personal, and sexual in nature. Joyce began to
feel more fully understood and connected to these men than to
her own husband, who in comparison seemed too dull, needy,
and demanding. Nights on the computer gradually became
Joyce's primary source of excitement and distraction, as they
began to include masturbation and sexual chat. In the morning,
she'd drag herself off to work, and by evening she was often
too tired to even help with family meals. In the evenings, she
frequently nodded off for a couple of hours in front of the TV.
But when her husband went to sleep, Joyce came to life again
on the computer. Roy, thinking that Joyce was ill or stressed
out, kept suggesting she take some time off from work or see
a doctor to find out why she was so tired and why she had
lost interest in their lovemaking. Joyce said it was the busy tax
season at work so she couldn't take time off, and although she
agreed to make an appointment with her doctor, she somehow
never got around to it.

Joyce never let on about her nightly liaisons, believing them
to be personal fantasies, unrelated to her marital relationship,

just as the romance novels had been. In time, one of Joyce's online chat partners mentioned that he was going on a business trip to her city and suggested an offline meeting. Filled with a mixture of fear and excitement, Joyce met and had sex with this man at his hotel. This behavior rapidly escalated into a pattern of having sexual chats and masturbation with more men online, which led to sexual encounters with several of those partners offline. Joyce's secret fantasy life came to a crashing end several months later when her husband confronted her after he caught a sexually transmitted disease from her.

∾

JOYCE WAS A cybersex user who became addicted to the intense arousal she experienced in her fantasy life. Her story did not have a happy ending: Her husband of fourteen years, feeling betrayed and outraged, filed for divorce. After almost losing custody of her three children, Joyce finally sought help and began the lengthy process of rebuilding her shattered life.

WHEN YOUR SEXUAL INTERESTS CAUSE YOU SHAME

TODAY ENDLESS WEB sites tout the virtues of nearly every fetish and alternative form of sexual expression and lifestyle. For those seeking reassurance that they are not alone in their specific area of sexual fascination, the multiplicity of images and information easily found online can help decrease shame by educating, reducing isolation, and providing connections to communities of others with similar sexual interests. Some men and women, not previously exposed to nontraditional sexual content pre-Internet, can be caught relatively unaware of the diversity of their own sexual interests and feelings.

Finding yourself aroused or interested in an unusual or different type of sexual stimulus that had previously hardly occurred to you can cause confusion, fear, shame, secrecy, and self-judgment. Some question whether these sexual feelings are "normal" or "healthy." Partners, confused by the introduction of an unknown factor into their primary relationship, want to make sense of it all. The question then is, when does curiosity, novelty, and a positive addition to one's sexual enjoyment cross the line into a problem?

Taking into account the need to avoid judgment of people's feelings and interests and individual sexual arousal patterns, there are still situations that call out for intervention and evaluation. Some of these are:

- *Self Hatred* If you despise yourself for certain sexual feelings and interests, or having them makes you feel hopeless, help is needed. While getting help might not change or eliminate these feelings or interests, it will help you gain insight into yourself and find ways to understand and live more comfortably with who you are. Trying to eliminate parts of yourself through self-hatred, denial, or self-diagnosis, even if you find them amoral or unacceptable from a religious standpoint, is usually not successful and can bring about depression, anxiety, and a host of other mental health problems. It is unhealthy to think that you are not lovable by others or by God because you have certain sexual feelings or behaviors. If you or a loved one has sexual feelings that are abhorrent to you, it is important to get informed help. The American Association of Sex Educators, Counselors and Therapists (www.aasect.org) and The Society for the Advancement of Sexual Health (www.sash.net) Web sites list professionals by geographic region who are trained to help sort out these kinds of concerns. For religious persons, the Resources section lists faith-based resources.

- *Lying and Secrecy* If you are lying to a spouse or significant other about some area of your sexuality, even if you have not acted upon it, it is unfair to your partner and is likely to damage your relationship. For example, it is an invitation to relational problems to look at porn material (whether same-sex, fetish, or some other sexual fascination) which your spouse would be shocked to find on your computer. A fear often expressed by people with sexual secrets, especially those with sexual secrets from a partner, is "If he or she knew what I like to do or want to do, they would leave me." In fact, more spouses leave because they have been lied to and kept in the dark than because something has been honestly brought up to them to discuss. If you are too ashamed or fearful to let your partner in on your secrets then get help from a trained counselor or religious professional who can help you figure this out.

- *Fetish Dependency* Some people cannot become aroused or function sexually without the inclusion of some or all aspects of a fetish object or behavior. While this may not be a problem for those comfortable incorporating this kind of sexuality into their lives, in some cases their partners may sense an absence of reciprocity and affection and may feel objectified in the sexual relationship. Other people may find their unusual sexual interests unacceptable to themselves. If you cannot function sexually without including some fetishistic behavior which is unacceptable to you or a partner, then clearly a problem exists that needs to be addressed with the help of a trained professional.

- *Spousal Rejection* How you adjust to having nontraditional sexual feelings or interests depends greatly on your marital/relationship status. Single people may seek out partners with similar sexual interests or patterns for dating and sex and inform any new partners about

these important aspects of themselves. These days
the Internet provides you easy access to people with
similar interests, making it more possible to find and
date someone like yourself. However, even if you have
become accepting of these sexual feelings, it is quite
a different matter to bring those thoughts, ideas, and
behaviors into a preexisting relationship with someone
who does not know about or share them. Some also
feel that acting out some of these behaviors in a primary
relationship, even if accepted by their spouse, would
be uncomfortable and false at best. Again, while this is
clearly problematic, the solution is not keeping secrets
and hiding behaviors from a loved one. With secrets
and hidden behavior there can be no meaningful
intimacy. It is important in these types of situations to
make use of marital and/or spiritual counselors to help
find a sexual life that both people who love each other
can accept and respect.

- *Partner Inequality* While some spouses and partners
  may initially accept or go along with an unfamiliar or
  uncomfortable sexual behavior in order to keep the
  peace or keep the family together, this situation almost
  always proves violating to the consenting spouse. For
  the partner who holds the alternative sexual interest, this
  is often, at best, unsatisfying. Spouses of people with a
  fetish or alternative sexual lifestyle need to be very clear
  with themselves about their beliefs and boundaries and
  most importantly, be willing to openly communicate
  their feelings. Because you fear losing a relationship
  doesn't mean you have to go through with some sexual
  act that makes you feel bad about yourself or your
  spouse or goes against your beliefs.
- *Inability to Change* Some people are committed to
  changing some unacceptable aspect of their sexuality
  (fetish, same-sex interest) and have found themselves

unable to do so no matter how they have tried. They then become depressed, self-hating, or worse. Although it is not likely that your sexual desires can be significantly altered, there are ways to manage and deal with your choices of sexual behaviors and lifestyle. Again, opening yourself up to a neutral professional, whose primary goal is to help you find peace of mind and health, will be a good first step toward health.

- *Consequences* If you are experiencing or are risking negative consequences (health, legal, relationship, career) related to a sexual behavior or interest, it is important to talk to about it and get help. If you persist in sexual behaviors or activities that have caused or have the potential to cause harm to yourself and others, you may have an addiction or be developing one. Get help now.

SAME-SEX INVOLVEMENT

UNFORTUNATELY ONE OF the many misconceptions about people who are interested in or actually do have sex with someone of the same sex is that "that must mean they are gay." These issues are understandably perplexing to someone in a primary heterosexual relationship with such a person. Tina helps us understand her fears:

I always sort of knew that my husband had some interest in men sexually, even just in the way that he looked at a good-looking guy who walked by, but I never paid much attention to it until the day I found all the gay porn on our computer. That scared me. I knew he looked at porn sometimes and masturbated, but that seemed normal to me and a part of our own private lives. But I had no idea the extent to which he had been looking at pictures and stories about men. When I realized this I immediately wondered whether or not he was really gay and if all we have shared together might come to an end. I was angry too, because I felt like this secret should never have been kept from me.

❧

IT IS IMPORTANT to have better understanding of those who have same-sex interest or behavior but pursue sex and relationships with opposite sex partners. Reasons why a man or woman might be sexually aroused by members of the same sex include:

BISEXUALITY The person is sexually aroused to differing degrees by same- and opposite-sex partners

SEXUAL SHAME OR EMBARRASSMENT The person seeks same-sex experiences because they feel that what they want to do sexually is too shameful or embarrassing to ask of their spouse or partner. For example, the man who strongly wants to be sexually dominated, but feels that it would be wrong to ask this of a woman, may look to another man to act out this particular fantasy or fetish.

SEEKING INTENSITY Sex addicts seek sexual intensity as a means of emotional control and escape. A sex addict may act out with a same-sex partner because that behavior brings with it—for them—the kind of increased "forbidden intensity" they seek.

SEXUAL OPPORTUNITY Someone might be in a situation (military, school, prison) where access to their choice of partner is unavailable, so they turn to same-sex experiences because that is what is available to them.

SEXUAL COMMERCE Someone might seek out or enact same-sex experiences because they are paid to do so.

SEXUAL TRAUMA Someone might have had certain traumatic sexual abuses in childhood that they "reenact" under certain situations or stressors. For example, the married man who was sexually abused by a stepfather now seeks out sexual images online of older men with younger men, though he has no sexual interest in either one when seeing them on the street.

∾

REGARDLESS OF WHY Theresa's husband might have same-sex arousal or interests, the more immediate problem for their marriage is that he has been keeping all of this a secret from her. While it would have been healthy for her to respond to her feelings about his sexual interests earlier by discussing this with him, his ongoing secrecy is a real violation of their commitment to each other. While he might or might not have a porn or sex addiction, it is essential that he is willing to be completely honest with her about his feelings and experiences and that they seek some professional help to sort through the confusion and challenges that these situations can create.

PORNOGRAPHY AND SEX ADDICTION IN GAY MEN AND LESBIANS

I think I have a sex addiction problem. I compulsively masturbate to Internet porn and hook up through the gay chat rooms. This has been going on for over three years.

❧

A PORN- OR SEX-ADDICTED gay man or woman is not compulsively sexual because of a same-sex orientation, but rather because of his or her own personal psychological and emotional problems. This is the same of heterosexuals who are sexually addicted. The same problems and healing paths discussed throughout this book are as applicable to gays as they are to straight people.

However, gay men and women do live in a subculture that—unfortunately for the gay pornography, sex, and love addict—emphasizes sexual freedoms rather than sexual boundaries. The gay culture's greater acceptance of sexual expression leaves gay sex addicts with less opportunity for self-examination and little support for behavior change.

Some use being gay as a cloak to mask the addictive nature of their sexual and relational behaviors, justifying their intense sexual focus and sexual acting out as a part of being a gay man or lesbian, accusing anyone who challenges them on it as being homophobic or not understanding them. This is their denial. Others will blame their problem behavior on being perennially single, on their unhappy relationship, on their stressful job, and so on. This blaming or denial process keeps the sex addict from taking responsibility for the real problem, that of the sexual behavior itself.

Sex addiction is not a homosexual problem; it is just as profound and problematic for heterosexuals. For example, heterosexual male sex addicts act out in many of the same ways as gay men do; they just have different venues and choose a different gender to play with. Gay men go to sex clubs, straight men go to strip clubs; gay men go to bathhouses, straight men hire prostitutes and go to motels. Both may end up at adult bookstores. There is a tremendous crossover of bisexual activity and transsexual acting out as well. Straight male sex addicts act out with as much intensity, secrecy, shame, and frequency as their gay counterparts.

Lesbian sex and romance addicts share with some heterosexual women long histories of unhealthy, impulsive relationship seeking, often bonding too quickly with abusive or unavailable partners. In 12-step meetings and group therapy for sexual and relationship addictions, gay and straight men and women often work side by side in the same groups, as they have more in common discussing the difficult feelings underlying their problem sexual and relationship experiences than the superficial differences they have regarding their sexual orientation.

Unfortunately, some closeted or sadly self-hating bisexual or gay men seek treatment for pornography and "sex addiction" or attend sex addiction 12-step programs because they want to rid themselves of their same-sex arousal feelings and activities. The only way they can tolerate these same-sex feelings and activities interest are by pathologizing them—that is, convincing themselves that they are sick. These men enter treatment to eliminate their sexual acting out, but with a homophobic focus. They want to "recover" from their same-sex desire, interest, and involvements, which they label as "sex addiction." For these troubled men, the label "sex addict" is an easier and less challenging way of managing their unacceptable same-sex feelings and interests than facing and accepting their own bisexuality or homosexuality. Some of these men remain in tortured marriages and or drift from heterosexual relationship to heterosexual relationship, hating themselves for not being able to truly "get sober" which to them would mean no longer having same-sex fantasies, desires, or behaviors. This has nothing to do with sex addiction. Good therapy or 12-step recovery and healing from sexual addiction has nothing to do with changing one's sexual orientation.

❧

WITHOUT INSIGHT, THERE is no change; without change, there is no healing.

Without recovery, all addictions continue despite adverse consequences. Only when the consequences are severe enough do most addicts seek help. This stage is often referred to as "bottoming out." Each type of addiction has its own particular consequences. The losses that pathological gamblers experience are typically financial. Alcoholics experience many health consequences, even before they have problems in their relationships or jobs. Sex addicts experience relationship problems, job loss, public shaming, arrests and imprisonment, sexually transmitted diseases, and—for women sex addicts—unwanted pregnancies. These consequences will be described in greater detail in the next chapter.

Whether driven by the desire to "have it all" without any consequences or as a part of an addictive pattern, people who make intensely arousing pleasurable distractions a primary life priority tend to lose the ability to see reality clearly, often to the detriment of relationships, other forms of recreation, and health. They lose touch with an emotional tool vital for mental health: the ability to be objective, to stand back from any situation and evaluate potential outcomes *before* choosing to jump into it. For those compulsively driven to use sexual images and content for distraction, the rational and self-reflective ability that allows healthy people to make good choices has been replaced by a relationship with pornography and the arousal that it provides.

This separation from reality, maintained through denial, rationalization, blaming others, and justification, prevents them from seeing the results, outcome, or consequences of their behaviors. Loved ones are angry and hurt, finances are ruined, jobs or even lives are lost, they may even get arrested, but often porn abusers/addicts do not see their sexual behavior as being the source of the problem. Feeling justified or entitled, or blaming others for their unhappiness, they can literally misperceive reality. Without help and intervention, the only relationship to which the addict holds any real allegiance is to the sexual activity and the distraction it provides.

In this chapter we have defined how some people may integrate pornography into their sexual health, while others simply abuse it, using fantasy and porn to compulsively escape their emotions and lives. We have offered signs that can help to identify abusive and addictive sexual behavior, and have also taken a look at the types of people who can get tangled up in the lure of the Net. The next chapter will offer insight into how people can justify their sexual acting out to themselves and those around them, while ignoring its troubling effects.

CHAPTER 3

OUT OF CONTROL

WHILE THE MEN and women who abuse pornography and sexual fantasy to the point of harming themselves and others may appear functional in many other areas of their lives, they are clearly out of touch with the consequences of their sexual behavior. Despite obvious warning signs, they will place sex at the top of their priority list, a choice that often has serious costs in every area of their lives. This chapter will examine the inner worlds of porn abusers and sex addicts, using their own words and stories to offer insight into their misguided thinking and actions.

I am undergoing a divorce because of multiple extra-marital affairs I have had that originated with Internet porn. I don't want to lose yet another relationship to this behavior, but don't know if I can stop.

I am sexually addicted to porn on the Internet with constant masturbation. I am tired of living in a fantasy world and want a real relationship. Where do I begin?

THE POWER OF DENIAL

THOSE WHO USED porn and sexual behaviors isolate themselves from life and health, seeming to not comprehend the negative consequences of their behaviors until the worst happens. *This is their denial.* It is almost as if they refuse to see, or are unable to understand, the effect of their image-oriented sexual activity on themselves and those who love them. *This is their lack of empathy.* Unlike healthy people who sooner or later become aware of a looming problem, those caught up in patterns of impulsive and compulsive self-gratification find ways to ignore the seriousness of their actions, in order to continue doing them. Thus they minimize the consequences, avoid responsibility for their own actions, and rationalize what to anyone else is obviously problematic behavior. Those who become progressively hooked on going to adult bookstores and theaters, collecting and compulsively masturbating to porn, and are sexually addicted to porn and cyberporn have a great deal of denial.

Denial subtly insinuates itself into the mind, encouraging problem behaviors and increasingly separating from reality the person who is acting out. Those obsessed with pornography don't originally intend to ruin a marriage, abandon a career, or get arrested. Yet, often, they end up in these very circumstances, arriving there by incrementally becoming more involved with the intensity and arousal of their porn use, while justifying their behavior at each step of the way. As their isolated sexual activity escalates, they become less able and less willing to see the connection between their increasing personal problems and a solitary, hidden sex life. Highly impulsive and addicted pornography users are often deaf to the complaints, concerns, and criticisms of those around them, even those they love, and will often devalue, dismiss, and blame those who try to point out the problem. Nor, unbelievably, will they respond to their increasingly neglected careers, family lives, or even lack of sleep! Those who use porn and cybersex as a way to cope and escape life's challenges will write off or dismiss these clear warning signs by accusing anyone trying to intervene of nagging, being prudish and restrictive, or of asking too much of them. They will say that you just don't understand them. They do this to protect their unrestricted access to their sexual highs, leaving partners and loved ones feeling unheard and disregarded in the process.

TYPES OF DENIAL

AS NOTED IN Chapter Two, the excitement and intensity of pornography itself, particularly when used online, combined with the hidden and potentially addictive nature of emotionally arousing behaviors, create for some people an extraordinarily powerful, internal drug-like state that becomes increasingly more desirable to attain. But in order to protect unlimited access to the resources (computer, DVDs, magazines, time alone, Internet), they must find ways to convince both themselves and loved ones why they are so involved with these experiences and so unavailable elsewhere. This escalates the problem, making it more difficult for users and those around them to ascertain what is actually going wrong. Denial takes many forms:

Entitlement

I just said to myself, "Look how hard I am working. I give to the family, the company, working nights and some weekends too. There really is no time left for me. There is no time when I can just do what I want to do without interruption or obligation to others. I deserve a little pleasure in life too! If I spend a few hours here and there online, getting myself off on a little fantasy, it is my only reward for all the work that I do and all that I give to others."

—JEFF, A 51-YEAR-OLD MARRIED EXECUTIVE
WITH TWO CHILDREN; FIRED AFTER THREE
WRITTEN WARNINGS NOT TO LOOK AT INTERNET
PORN SITES AT WORK

Minimization

I figured I was no different. So many of my friends are involved in this Internet thing too. They go online, meet guys for dates, have sex, and then brag about it the next day. My behavior is similar to what I read about in the newspaper or watch on the TV news. Besides, I have been single a long time. While I wait for a relationship, I might as well get all I can. I am not in danger; I can handle myself. Anyone I meet online at least has the money for a computer and the knowledge to use one so I'm not going to meet any maniacs, right? Besides, I can tell when someone is too weird or into drugs from the kinds of things they write me.

—SAM, A 31-YEAR-OLD MAN,
"FOUND HIMSELF" GOING TO STRANGERS' HOUSES
TO HAVE SEX FOUR TO FIVE NIGHTS A WEEK
AFTER MEETING THEM ONLINE

∾

Justification

I kept telling myself, "This is what single men do." If I'm not in a relationship, then I need some kind of sexual excitement. I'm just going to the adult bookstores and collecting porn videos. I spend less money on this than on the lousy dating relationships I have been in the last year anyway. Besides, it's a whole lot better than sitting around some singles bar. When I leave work I have something to look forward to. The movies offer some excitement and distraction without ever having to leave my apartment. You can't beat that.

—DARRYL, A 24-YEAR-OLD SINGLE BANK CLERK WHO WAS SPENDING TWO TO THREE HOURS DAILY AFTER WORK IN THE ADULT VIDEO PORN BOOTHS AND BOTH WEEKEND DAYS IN HIS APARTMENT WATCHING PORN FILMS.

Blame

I just told my wife that this is what guys do, and thought, who wouldn't be buying magazines and videos with the lousy sex life I have at home? Ever since the babies were born we never have time and she has put on so much weight. Even when we were having sex, it wasn't anywhere as exciting or interesting as the women I see in films and talk to in the online chats and conversations I get into. Some of these women are really wild and I get to explore some things I can't even talk about at home.

—FRANK, A 31-YEAR-OLD MAN

Rationalization

This is how I looked at it: I'm not having affairs like other women I know and I am not even flirting with the doctors at work, though I know some other nurses who do. If I get online to have my secret little intrigues, no one really gets hurt and nothing becomes of it. Lots of women read romance novels or watch soap operas and they aren't doing anything wrong, so why am I?

—SUZANNE, A 36-YEAR-OLD NURSE WHO, AFTER CHATTING ONLINE WITH A STRANGER FOR FOUR MONTHS, LEFT HER MARRIAGE OF SEVEN YEARS TO BE WITH HIM. HER HUSBAND NEVER EVEN KNEW THAT SHE USED THE COMPUTER.

DESPITE THE POWER and excitement they experience online, the most consistent emotion described by most porn and cyberporn abusers, that reinforces most of the forms of denial described above, is an underlying feeling of hopelessness. On some level, even though their compulsive sexual activities are clearly harming others, most of these people feel somehow that *they are a victim.* No matter the actual life circumstances of the pornography abuser or cybersex addict, when justifying their sexual activity to themselves, most will say that they felt at the mercy of the problems or people in their lives without much sense of control over them, and that sexual acting out gave them a sense of freedom and power they did not feel elsewhere.

These men and women, often repeating patterns of interaction learned in emotionally neglectful childhoods, feel burdened by what seem to them the unceasing demands of others, especially those close to them, for attention, participation, validation, and support. Not surprisingly, they find it difficult to know their own emotional needs and nearly impossible to ask directly for them to be met. Even if they stop using sex to quell anxiety and to cope, it is likely that without some kind of outside help they will eventually find themselves searching for some other means of escaping what they experience as their painfully unmet needs, while continuing to fear and avoid what feel like the oppressive bonds of intimate relationships.

THE CONSEQUENCES OF SEXUAL OBSESSION

MOST SHORT-TERM, IMMEDIATELY gratifying, pleasurable activities (sex included) have the potential to be used obsessively or even become addictive, but the accessibility, affordability, anonymity, and interactive capability of cybersex makes it a particularly arousing and potentially addictive experience. Compulsive use of online sex also creates consequences that affect significant others, families, and children, stemming specifically from the sexual content of the user's Internet addiction. Here are some typical consequences of addictive cybersex use:

- Isolation from dating, social interaction, and the potential to meet available romantic partners (single people)
- Reduced intimacy, sexuality, and communication with one's committed partner. Increased guilt and shame about covering up the cybersex activities
- Repeated lies and justifications about sexual activities, and repeated promises to stop or change
- Mistrust and betrayal
- Potential job loss—more likely for cybersex activities at work than for nonsexual workplace online use
- Contracting a sexually transmitted disease (STD) from live physical contact with anonymous partners met online
- Risk of infecting spouses and significant others with STDs
- Loss of self-esteem and self-worth by partners trying to "measure up" to fantasy porn images or lovers

- Exposing children to pornography when it is left around the house, when they step into the room where a parent is involved in cybersex activities, or find pornography on the computer
- Ignoring or emotionally neglecting children and family because of an obsession with images and online sex

HOW DO I KNOW WHEN I HAVE HIT BOTTOM?

PEOPLE OFTEN FIRST seek help when their sexual behaviors create serious problems in some other area of their lives. Unfortunately, as we have suggested, often only when the consequences of some sexual behavior become severe does the person "wake up" to the obvious problems they have created. In fact, most are more often roused out of their sexual stupor by some external consequence than by responding to any thought or feeling that they should stop. Emotional problems, neglect of health and self-care, relationship blowups, sexual problems, career difficulties, family dysfunction, legal problems, and financial difficulties can be the more far-reaching results of a person's substitution of images for true intimacy.

Emotional Problems

I felt guilt and shame that led to isolation and loneliness. This was a part of my life I could not (did not want to) share with my wife. It drove a wedge between us. I was depressed at times because I felt trapped and unable to break free from this obsession. It was scary.

—A 45-YEAR-OLD MARRIED MAN

While I wasted many hours at the theaters and bookstores, it never seemed to really satisfy me. Oh, it would for the moment or while I was actually viewing the movies, but the letdown and guilt afterwards were a real downer. I found myself risking everything—wife, family, and reputation—in pursuit of this compulsion. It was when I began to view it as a compulsion that I knew I had a serious problem. But even then I did not and could not stop.

—A 47-YEAR-OLD MARRIED MAN

Cybersex use consumed my life. I was to the point where just closing my eyes would bring on an uncontrollable need to feed my addictive fantasies. The pictures I viewed would haunt me day and night. I couldn't look at another person without some filthy thought coming into my mind.

—A 35-YEAR-OLD MARRIED WOMAN

∾

THOSE OBSESSED WITH pornography face the emotional challenge of living a double life. Keeping secrets, telling lies, minimizing and altering situations and circumstances to cover up reality, and lying to yourself—these are the realities of constant acting out. Some feel as if they are living two lives: a hidden one taking place in a virtual reality of pictures, film, and online, and another lived in the real world. Their sexual life is one of fantasy, arousal, and distraction where endless possibilities abound for intrigue, flirtation, and sexual distraction. Time does not really exist when you're watching movie after movie or lost to searching the Internet for sex. This effect is similar to what happens to a compulsive gambler in a casino.

For those heavily involved with cybersex, the world is a never-ending ride with something or someone new always waiting just a mouse-click away.

Absorption in so much distraction, arousal, and fantasy, while at the same time trying to manage the responsibilities, disappointments, and challenges of the real world creates a gap that widens each day. As the sexual acting out continues, the porn user becomes increasingly irritable, controlling, withdrawn, and exhausted. By the time they seek help, many are anxious, depressed or both, driven by ongoing fears of being found out, underlying shame, despair, and for some, self-hatred. Whereas most users report having gotten into porn as a means of seeking excitement and distraction from their problems, they later found that what they were doing actually created more serious problems than it resolved.

Neglect of Self-Care and Health

As these behaviors progress, there is less and less time for good self-care and physical maintenance. Being up long after others have gone to bed or rising in the middle of the night to access soft-core cable movies or sex on the Internet causes exhaustion and a loss of healthy boundaries. "I'll just look for a few more minutes" turns into hours as they search for the next perfect image or person with whom to chat or masturbate. In order to avoid confrontations from a concerned spouse or being caught in the act with a sexual or romantic partner online, some porn addicts give up precious sleep time for sexual activity; others, anxious about what they are doing, find their formerly healthy sleep patterns increasingly disrupted by anxiety and fear.

Besides sleep, other aspects of physical health may suffer. The Internet chat environment creates an atmosphere of immediacy and intensity in which concerns about safety and self-care are forgotten. Often, resolution of this intense arousal state can be satisfied only by offline (real-life) encounters with casual partners, some of whom may be dangerous people or may be infected with sexually transmitted diseases. Here are two men's stories:

❧

I shudder when I recall the risks I took during my active sex addiction. More than once, arriving at a stranger's home at midnight after chatting online for more than two hours, I'd be excited and filled with anticipation. With no condom available, I'd put aside my "usual cautions" of safe sex and have unprotected oral and anal sex; health considerations did not even enter my mind. However, as I walked out of the stranger's home, I was immediately filled with fear and self-loathing, wondering if I'd have to pay a terrible price for this impulsive sexual encounter. I never had much time to think about my HIV risk, I was more focused on the immediate problem of explaining my 2 AM arrival to my partner waiting at home.

—CHARLES, A 44-YEAR-OLD MAN IN A
TEN-YEAR COMMITTED RELATIONSHIP

Stopping off at the adult bookstore after work never seemed like a betrayal of my marriage. I got off from work hours earlier than Susan and I would always be home, often ready with dinner by the time she got there. It was only when I starting letting the other men there provide me with oral sex that I got really scared. I really don't even think I'm bisexual. I was just so jazzed up by the intensity of going there, hiding my car out back and looking at the images for hours. At some point I just wanted a release and didn't care who gave it to me or if I used a condom. I stopped having sex with [my partner] Susan because I felt so ashamed of what I had done with the men that I couldn't allow myself to be with her and I was afraid I could infect her with something. I just claimed that I was "tired" but she knew better. She started checking my finances and schedule until she figured out that something was going on. The night I finally told her what was up was one of the worst nights of my life. But I also see that night as the beginning of my healing.

—FRANKLIN, A 52-YEAR-OLD
MARRIED ENGINEER

ᔕ

ALTHOUGH PEOPLE CAN'T get a sexually transmitted disease from viewing porn at home or having online sex, in one survey 40 percent of those addicted to cybersex reported eventually progressing to real-life sexual encounters, often including unsafe sex. [9]

ᔕ

Problems with Relationships, Intimacy, and Sexuality

It created a wall between my wife and me. I avoided intimate conversation so I wouldn't have to answer any questions that would reveal those secretive and shameful events. As for our intimate relationship, all the sex with myself resulted in less sex with my wife. My preoccupation with body parts on the screen transferred into a preoc-

cupation with body parts of real people. My wife became older and less attractive to me with every young person I saw on the screen.

—A 64-YEAR-OLD MARRIED MAN

∾

CONSISTENT AND EXCESSIVE abuse of pornography, with or without masturbation, can produce tremendously destructive consequences for those in a committed relationship. Obsession with cyberporn, online images, video exchange, or other isolating masturbatory activity on the part of one partner leaves relationships flat and drained of meaning for both. Sexuality, affection, honesty, and bonding all suffer, as the porn abuser becomes increasingly fixated on his or her solo and anonymous sexual experiences. Spouses and significant others, often in the dark about the problem and confused by the emotional and physical distancing of the one who is sexually acting out, can blame themselves for their relationship problems and often judge themselves sexually or physically inadequate to meet their partner's needs.

∾

It affected our sexual relationship greatly. My sexual energy was "saved" for the porn. I lost interest in sex at home because I knew there were an unlimited amount of pictures on the Internet that could "get me off" anytime I preferred. My wife sensed the distance between us. Previously, it was being "connected with each other" that formed the basis for our intimate relationship, and this in turn led to sexual activity. But because we weren't connected emotionally any longer, we rarely had sex. When we did, it was more of an activity to get through than an intimate connection.

—A 45-YEAR-OLD MARRIED MAN

My husband could no longer satisfy me. I wanted what I saw in the videos and pictures, and was too embarrassed to ask him for it.

—A 35-YEAR-OLD MARRIED WOMAN

ᵔ

ONLINE RELATIONSHIPS (OFTEN rationalized as "not really an affair") can be easily denied to a spouse in such statements as "I have never even met her, how can you say I am cheating?" or "We have never touched each other and certainly have never had sex, it's just a playful distraction, so what's the big deal?" yet these betrayals are often acutely painful to the spouse left behind. Here is what one man's partner told us:

He's never been physically unfaithful, but nonetheless I feel cheated on. I never know who or what he is thinking of when we are intimate. How can I compete with hundreds of anonymous others who are now in our bed, in his head? When he says something sexual to me in bed, I wonder if he has said it to others, or if it is even his original thought. Now our bed is crowded with countless faceless strangers, where once we were intimate. With all this deception, how do I know he has quit, or isn't moving into other behaviors?

〜

ANOTHER WOMAN RELATED:

My husband is using sexual energy that should be used with me. The person on the other end of that computer is live and is participating in a sexual activity with him. They are doing it together and are responding to each other. It is one thing to masturbate to a two-dimensional screen image. But to engage in an interactive sexual encounter means that you are being sexual with another person, and that is cheating.

〜

RELATIONSHIPS SUFFER TRAGIC consequences when cyber affairs turn into offline "real" sexual affairs or encounters. Those discovered to be sexually acting out on the Internet often must deal with a partner's sense of betrayal, loss of self-esteem, anger, depression, distancing, and even ending of the relationship. Upcoming chapters will explore in greater detail how compulsive cybersex affects the relationship between committed couples.

Disruption of Family Life

In relationships where compulsive porn use is routine for one of the partners, family life suffers. Basic responsibilities of childcare and involvement in family activities become secondary to the pornography or cyberporn and its resulting emotional distractions and physical exhaustion.

Now having dealt with his problem, William reflects on the past:

I was spending less and less time playing with the children after school and on weekends and I had been such an active dad before all this started. Instead of joining the family after work, I would hole up in the den on the computer until late in the evening, sometimes skipping dinner altogether. I gradually got less involved in figuring out the usual household dilemmas, the childcare balancing act, or even helping with the kids' homework. I can see how my wife picked up the slack, taking on more of my responsibilities. When she would challenge me, I would lie and defend myself, saying stuff like, "You don't seem to understand how important it is for me to get this work done," or "Why can't you do your part and keep things out of my way so that I can work in here?" Sometimes I think I even picked fights to justify going in my study and shutting the door on her. It makes me feel really shameful when I think about it.

My wife tells me now that sometimes she was concerned about even leaving the kids with me when she went out to run errands. I would get so involved with whatever I was doing on the computer or watching porn in our bedroom, she worried that I wasn't really watching them and wouldn't hear if they needed me. And forget about any closeness between us! Making any kind of time for the two of us wasn't even on my radar. My denial about the whole thing only broke down when she finally confronted me and threatened to move out with the kids unless things changed. At that point I got honest about what I had really been doing and begged her to forgive me. When she insisted on my going to counseling, I finally agreed that there was a problem.

∾

COMPULSIVE USE OF pornography affects all aspects of parenting. In the previous story, William's attention was elsewhere. Read on to see how a porn user's inattention to his children may cost him his marriage:

I started buying movies and videos while we were pregnant with Jessica, and it just got worse after she was born. I think I really missed out on the special things like her first steps and words. I would spend hours locked in my home office at night either watching the movies or on the computer. Many days were spent catching up on sleep, missing out on time with our child.

The event that caused our separation was when I actually neglected Jessica one day while I was having cybersex. I was supposed to listen to the baby monitor while my wife went to work. Somehow I left the monitor in another room, thinking I would just turn on the computer for a few minutes. Before I knew it, several hours had passed. My wife came home to find me masturbating in front of the computer and our daughter, having broken one of her toys, screaming her head off alone in her room. My wife took our daughter and left me the next day.

Now that we are separated, I spend more time with Jessica than I did before, because when I go to see her, I am really being with her, not just passing time to get back to the computer.

—FRANK, 33 YEARS OLD AND SEPARATED AFTER
AN EIGHT-YEAR MARRIAGE

∾

IN EVEN MORE concerning cases, children are directly exposed to pornography:

I know the boys have found some of the porn I have hidden around the house. Once I found one of my magazines under my 11-year-old's mattress but felt too ashamed to speak to him or my wife about it. I just put it back in the drawer. I know that the boys have walked in while I was online, sometimes seeing the sexual chat rooms where I spend time. They've even told me to "take those pictures off the computer," that "it's gross." I think they've lost respect for me.

—ARMAND, A 42-YEAR-OLD MAN, MARRIED
SEVENTEEN YEARS

∿

EVEN IF CHILDREN are not exposed to pornography, or do not know how their caregiver is spending his or her time, they are harmed by the caregiver's emotional unavailability. Pornography abuse and sex addiction encourage isolation, parental tension, and arguments. Denial and blame prevent the porn and cybersex abuser from seeing the family consequences or their real part in them.

∿

WORK AND CAREER

KEEPING A PORN collection in your drawer at work or searching on your office computer for sexual encounters and hardcore pornography are dangerous business. Most companies, large and small, now have written rules regarding such behavior. Human resources policies usually include a verbal and/or written warning for the first offense, followed by immediate dismissal for a recurrence. In denial of the potential consequences, people hooked on the thrill of looking at sexual material in the office will often excuse their behavior by telling themselves, "They won't find out it was me" or "This is no big deal, I look online only after hours, not on company time," or "Lots of employees do this, I have seen pictures on other people's computers a million times," or worse, "I always go in the bathroom stall during lunch to masturbate." Denial kicks in as they will try to get around memos and warnings rather than acknowledging and responding to them.

Raif, a 28-year-old married insurance investigator with a new baby at home was fired after only six months on a new job because of his workplace sexual behavior. He puts it this way:

> *Somehow I thought that I could get around the system by not looking at the porn at work but just downloading it there and burning it onto a CD. It got so I could start a download early in morning and have several hundred images to take home with me at the end of each day. I figured that even if I got caught, I could prove that I wasn't watching it at work. After they wrote me up the first time I tried downloading the porn through sites and portals that were not porn related, thinking that anyone watching wouldn't know what I was really doing, but I wasn't as smart as I thought I was. It turns out that the technology people at work easily tracked what I was doing and I got fired anyway.*

∿

IN THE PAST, some tolerant businesses looked the other way at such behavior. Now companies are actively monitoring and stopping cyberporn viewing and sexual chat in the work environment. Federal law permits an employer to review and read an employee's e-mail and to subject the e-mail's author to scrutiny and reproach. Computers networked into a mainframe or using a central ISDN line often have filters and screens designed to monitor the online activities of workers. Personal computers, laptops, PDAs, and even cellular phones are now routinely checked when in maintenance or while having software upgrades. Those employees unable or unwilling to change their behaviors face dismissal:

After losing a good job when they found me cruising Internet sex sites at the office, I couldn't find anything I wanted to do and ended up spending all day at home looking at porn videos and magazines while my wife worked to keep our heads above water. In the last couple of years before we split up, I ran up about $9,000 on our credit cards in my "sexual adventures." My porn addiction cost me my marriage.

—A 39-YEAR-OLD MAN, NOW DIVORCED

He put both his job and mine in jeopardy. He did this by using my government computer account to surf online for porn during work hours. He had compiled more than 100 computer disks filled with alphabetized porn images, all downloaded during work hours, from that account before my boss finally called me aside to ask what this was all about.

—A 44-YEAR-OLD WOMAN, NOW SEPARATED

༄

OVER THE PAST several decades, human resources departments and employee assistance programs have become more knowledgeable about alcoholism and drug abuse, and have put systems into place to deal with employees whose alcohol or drug problem comes to light. These methods range from worker education to actual interventions on an employee's problem behaviors. They understand that warnings and slaps on the wrist are unlikely to cause behavior change in addicts who need more direct and immediate help and referrals to support groups like Alcoholics Anonymous. The same compassionate corporate intervention is unlikely to be available to the worker who brings sexual materials into the workplace or obtains them while there on work computers.

One company recently learned a hard lesson due to their lack of understanding about these types of problems. John, a 33-year-old physical therapist at a rehabilitation clinic, was discovered downloading pornography on his work computer. In line with company policy, he was given a written warning including a statement that if the problem recurred he'd be fired. The company's policy also included (1) no further Internet access for John at work, and (2) a note in his record as to what happened. But there were no recommendations for further evaluation or treatment for his sexual disorder. John wrote the following letter to his supervisor:

> *I am very sorry about my inappropriate behavior. It won't happen again. I want you to know that some years ago I had a similar problem at home. My wife found out and threatened to leave. I haven't looked at inappropriate Internet sites at home for quite a while. I really don't want anything on my record. How about if I voluntarily desist from Internet access instead?*

∾

THE SUPERVISOR DENIED his request and proceeded with the company's usual policy. John was officially denied Internet access at work.

Four months later one of John's young physical therapy

patients accused him of making sexual advances toward her while he was providing physical therapy. He was fired, and his institution ended up settling lawsuits with the patient for large sums of money to avoid these abuses by one of their employees going public.

Had John been immediately referred to counseling or seen the company's EAP (employee assistance professional) when his problem of going online for sex first appeared, there would have been a professional assessment and support that allowed a more *situation-appropriate* response toward John. This might have prevented the abuse that later occurred.

FINANCES

TRADITIONAL PORNOGRAPHY COLLECTIONS are expensive. Good porn magazines can retail for well over ten dollars, with some DVDs often costing ten times more. A sex addict who compulsively collects porn can end up purchasing hundreds of magazines and movies, leading to significant financial losses. One of the great benefits of the Internet is the low cost at which an endless amount of information and enjoyment can be accessed. This is in part why many have moved to access porn on the Internet. However, Internet porn has also provided enormous opportunities for people to benefit financially; for example, anyone who wishes to make money online can charge for access to their Web sites. In addition, Web sites run by "professionals" often provide more consistency and greater depth of content on specific types of pornography. Some of these, called *membership sites*, require the viewer to pay a monthly access fee. Other sites charge for the amount of time the user spends viewing materials and images.

The intensely arousing nature of the sexual content encourages the online porn viewer to keep looking and searching for more. This is highly expensive for the viewer and lucrative for the operators. It is not unusual for a site to charge several dollars per minute. In one sitting, some viewers can spend hundreds of dollars. Specialty sexual services such as live video feeds, live viewing of models, and sexual chats with models are also charged by the minute, in addition to the initial membership fees. Cell phone and PDA downloads are priced at several dollars and more per minute. Often porn addicts, momentarily feeling ashamed or angry with themselves for all the time and money spent online, will cancel memberships or even online access or throw away all of their porn. But within a few days they sign back on and start the process all over again. All of this can be very expensive. It is not unusual for someone to spend hundreds or even thousands dollars a month in this type of activity.

In addition to the direct costs of porn activity, compulsive online use can eat up large sums of money for computer upgrades and new equipment. If the online activities progress to telephone contact and offline encounters, the expenses mount quickly:

Even though I did not purchase anything online, I spent thousands of dollars on my addiction. I pushed my wife to let me spend some of our vacation money to upgrade my computer, which wasn't cheap as I wanted extra graphics capabilities, a larger hard drive, and a Webcam. I told her that this was all for my video game hobby. My wife wanted to wait until prices went down, but I insisted until she finally gave in.

—A 29-YEAR-OLD MAN, MARRIED FOUR YEARS

I spent money in traveling, buying other women gifts, purchasing phone cards, staying in motels, and buying lovers dinner—outlays which have drained our mutual finances. This has created financial and emotional stress for both of us and made her increasingly want independence.

—A 44-YEAR-OLD LESBIAN,
PARTNERED FOR FOUR YEARS

BREAKING THE LAW

ACCESS TO ILLEGAL sexual activities and content, practically nonexistent only a decade ago, is now readily available through the Internet. This type of material includes exchange of images of child pornography, graphic sexual violence, mutilation, bestiality, and "snuff photos" depicting murder. Unknown to the average online viewer, however, many of these sites are either monitored or managed by governmental watchdog agencies so that they can keep an eye out for sexual offenders. Larger online service providers such as America Online (AOL), EarthLink, and Sprint report to the government any person involved in such activities. Stories like the following are occurring with increasing frequency around the country.

Kevin had always felt aroused by looking at and being around young teens. For many years, girls aged eleven to fourteen had been a strong part of his sexual fantasy life. Throughout his twenties, while dating and enjoying sex with women his own age, Kevin recalled having "crushes" on much younger girls who were friends of his little sister. Though never actually acting upon these thoughts, he would use them as subjects for masturbation and sexual fantasy. Now in his early thirties, married, with toddlers of his own, Kevin had pushed these "Lolita" interests to the back of his psyche and was enjoying marriage and a pleasant sex life.

Because the pregnancy and birth of their third child was hard on his wife's health, Kevin ended up taking on the responsibilities of raising two small children and most of the financial burden as well. It wasn't long before the pressures of his family life, challenges at work, and the long hours of caring for his wife began to weigh on him. Initially on impulse, Kevin turned to the computer in the late evenings after his kids and wife were in bed. He soon found the ready availability of explicit sexual images and video online. His impulse to look quickly became a habit. Within weeks, Kevin was online until late at night, sometimes into the early hours of the morning.

Kevin soon discovered "teen photo galleries" and "young teen chats." At that point, his long-suppressed fantasy life became increasingly more real, as Kevin was for the first time exposed to actual images and stories about underage girls. Lulled by the safety of his home computer, Kevin only briefly considered the illegality of his actions as he explored child pornography over the Internet. Before long he was regularly downloading and masturbating to photos of young teenage girls, and going to chat rooms to exchange pornographic images with others. It never occurred to him that he was actually transporting child sexual images over state lines (a felony) or that someone could track him doing this.

What Kevin did not know is that several of the teen sites he visited were under regular observation by the FBI, the agency most closely monitoring Internet use, particularly the illegal exchange of child pornography. The inevitable knock at his door, seizure of his computer hard drive, and subsequent arrest came as a total shock to Kevin and his family. The evidence, when uncovered, included hundreds of legal pornographic images in the computer along with dozens of illegal photos of young teens in various states of compromise and exploitation. Kevin was charged and prosecuted as a sex offender for engaging in the traffic of child pornography across state lines. Convicted, Kevin went to jail.

∾

FOR THE VULNERABLE man or woman, the intensity and addictive qualities of Internet sex and intrigue can be compared to that of crack cocaine. In both cases, the addiction progresses rapidly, and so do the negative consequences. Using the voices of actual men and women who have become ensnared in a cybersex web, this chapter has outlined some of these consequences, which can include emotional, relationship, family, career, financial, and legal disaster.

Cyberporn is not the only cause of significant problems with online sexuality, however. For some vulnerable people, romance or the search for Prince Charming or Ms. Right, with or without outright sex, can also wreak havoc, destroying families, relationships and careers. The next chapter describes this concern and what it means for those involved in online sex and "romance."

CHAPTER 4

The Reality of Romance Online

THIS CHAPTER EXPLORES the nature of romantic love, how the technology of the computer fosters and perpetuates fantasy, and how those who become addicted to the search for romance or sex are likely candidates to get tangled in the Net. It also discusses the pitfalls of online dating.

The lure of the Internet is not limited to pornography and interactive sexual adventure. It also provides an open door to dating and romantic fantasy. Legitimate dating sites can be a very useful and healthy way of meeting new people, and if you will likely find this discussion useful.

Unfortunately, looking for romance online can also have serious negative consequences. Stories abound of men and women whose lives have become destabilized, of relationships broken up, and sometimes even of life lost as a result of a passionate online fantasy romance. This chapter will present a few such cases and explain how the Internet can so powerfully entangle those who previously had stable lives. Also discussed is the phenomenon of fantasy romance, an experience that leaves some people endlessly repeating patterns of looking for relationships and sex, but ending up lost and confused. Over time they become addicted to the rush and intensity of romantic intrigue and find themselves desperately searching for love in much the same way as some become hooked on cybersex and pornography.

Traditionally, men tend to be more attracted to pornography, whereas women tend to be more aroused by an experience of relating. This makes sense, in that men are more visually stimulated than women and are aroused by images. Women, in general, are more likely to be turned on by relationships and romance rather than pictures. Even female sex addicts are less likely than men to participate in behaviors such as viewing pornography, voyeurism, or anonymous sex, and are more likely to be found in chat rooms and bars, seeking an emotional connection that usually turns sexual. However, there *are* female sex addicts who view pornography, engage in one-night stands, and prefer power to romance, just as there are men who repetitively seek out the "perfect relationship" and whose focus is seduction rather than just sex. This chapter is about those troubled men and women.

∽

LET'S START WITH an all-too-common scenario:

My 58-year-old married sister says that she has fallen in love on the Internet with a man that she hasn't even met, and her husband is desperate. She wants to leave him, and has told him so, but the other guy hasn't yet invited her. Her son knows about this and is furious at her. Their whole family is in turmoil. What can I do?

∽

HOW TO UNDERSTAND a situation like this, where a (previously) reasonable person decides to leave their marriage and family for someone they haven't actually met? And sadly, when such a couple does finally meet, the outcome is likely to be disappointing. Consider the story of Annette, a 37-year-old divorced nurse, who was searching online for a long-term relationship:

When I met Kevin online, I was sure I'd finally found my soul mate. We worked in related fields and were both interested in the same things. It was so easy to "chat" with him—in a short time I felt I'd known him forever. Since I live in California and he lives in Delaware, it was several months before we actually met. We exchanged daily e-mails, sent each other our photographs, and talked on the phone a few times. Our messages did eventually contain some sexual innuendos, but nothing explicit. Finally, we agreed to meet for a weekend in Chicago. By then I believed I was in love with him.

We arranged to rendezvous at O'Hare Airport on a Friday evening and went out to dinner. Kevin was as good-looking as his picture, and I could tell he was pleased with what he saw as well. But as the meal progressed, I began to suspect that I had made a big mistake with this guy. Throughout dinner Kevin was controlling, overbearing, and consistently interrupted my comments. He insisted on ordering dinner for me without asking what I wanted and talked endlessly about his plans for our next meeting without even asking my opinion. While chain-smoking and consuming martinis nonstop, he waxed on about how I really was "the girl of his dreams" and that he "couldn't wait" until I moved closer to be with him. I began to feel increasingly uncomfortable with the intensity of his approach, especially considering we had never really met before!

Thankfully, I had suggested we stay in separate hotel rooms while we got to know each other and was glad to retreat to my own room at the end of the first evening—that is, until his first knock at the door at 1 AM. I was tired and apprehensive but let him in anyway as he appeared upset. He sat down and began talking about his last few relationships and how unhappy he had been. How he hoped that this time it would work out and I would be "the one." It was clear to me that he now quite drunk. He began to make sexual suggestions and asked if we could lie together and cuddle. As he became more insistent, I started to feel truly frightened for my safety and asked him to leave. It was only when I threatened to call security that he agreed to go back to his own room. Early the next morning, on the first plane home I could get, I tried to figure out how I had gotten myself into this situation in the first place.

୬

LOVE CONNECTIONS ARE easy and fun to make, but the nature of Internet communication encourages fantasy and downplays reality. If you are single and just looking to have fun or perhaps meet someone special, the only potential loss may be the time spent online or going out for endless coffee dates. But if all-consuming emotions push your better judgment aside, the stakes are higher and the risks to you are greater. If you are married or in a committed relationship and find yourself online searching and responding to relationship and sexual overtures, you risk losing a lot more than you are likely to gain.

MEETING ONLINE:
THE MEDIUM IS THE MESSAGE

IN OUR CULTURE, many are isolated by circumstance, lack of community, and the time constraints of work. Even living in a large city surrounded by masses of people doesn't seem to offer many opportunities to meet a potential romantic partner. Without a doubt, the Internet has become a major resource for meeting new people. You can meet up by participating in a chat room or discussion group devoted to some particular interest, or through a multitude of online dating services.

Finding someone online has its advantages. The Internet can quickly and inexpensively link you with someone who may be hundreds or thousands of miles away, which would likely not happen without an online connection. The current use of writing rather than speaking as the primary form of Internet communication can also be beneficial when meeting new people. In contrast to live encounters, first impressions on the Internet are based on what you have to say, not so much on what you look like. Given the huge emphasis in our culture on looks, it can be an enormous advantage if you are insecure about your looks to engage a potential romantic partner before meeting face-to-face. Another advantage is that online, you have plenty of time to express yourself as fully and as positively as possible. If you tend to be shy, live interactions can produce so much anxiety that your best self can be hard to show. The Internet, by contrast, offers more time to think about what you really want to say and to take in the response of a potential partner. If you aren't a big talker, especially when first dating, meeting someone online provides an opportunity to present yourself in the most positive light. This is particularly true for e-mail, which can be sent and downloaded at one's convenience.

Here are some other advantages of Internet introductions:

- Newspaper ads limit you to describing yourself in twenty or thirty words, while computer matching "profiles" allow a description of several hundred words in many different areas. This detailed information on each person's profile provides you and others looking for a mate with a fairly well rounded view of the other person before you even meet—provided you both are being honest. This is a big improvement over meeting someone new for the first time in a bar or club.
- The cost of computer matching is a small fraction of offline matchmaking services.

- If you live in the suburbs or a small town, the pool of potential Internet matches is much larger than you will find in your local community, as long as you are willing to travel.
- Participation in topic-focused chat rooms and e-mail lists introduces you to many other people with whom you already share similar interests.

∾

BECAUSE OF THE Internet's apparent anonymity, you will likely feel less inhibited communicating via e-mail and instant message (IM) than in person. IM is an Internet service that allows back and forth chatting between people much like a telephone conversation, only in print. As a result, it is often easier to express your feelings more openly and honestly. This more open sharing of emotions can lead to a sense of intimacy much more rapidly than in an offline relationship.

VIRTUAL LOVE: AN OBJECT LESSON

INTERNET DATING, WITH its built-in barriers to full knowledge of the other person, is a perfect setup for "falling in love." Sometimes the outcome of online fantasy romances is good; we have all heard stories of couples who met online and are living "happily ever after." Unfortunately, for every success story there is at least one of unhappiness or even danger. Stories range from failed expectations, to disrupted marriages and even violence.

A poignant tale of reality's inability to live up to fantasy was told by Meghan Daum in her first-person story in *The New Yorker* magazine, "Virtual Love." [10] Daum wrote of her online relationship with Pete, "I was a desired person, the object of a blind man's gaze ... He told me that he thought about me all the time, though we both knew that the 'me' in his mind consisted largely of himself." She became equally obsessed with him.

When after several months of e-mails Pete flew from California to New York to meet Meghan, it was a disaster: "He talked so much that I wanted to cry ... We strained for conversation ... It was all wrong. The physical world had invaded our space. I wanted Pete out of my apartment.... I berated myself for not liking him, for wanting to like him more than I had wanted anything in such a long time. I was horrified by the realization that I had invested so heavily in a made-up character.... If Pete and I had met at a party, we probably wouldn't have spoken to each other for more than ten minutes." Their months-long intense fantasy romance died as a result of a single real-life meeting.

COMPUTER DATING CAVEATS

WHAT WENT WRONG with Meghan and Pete's "relationship"? One possible explanation is that the medium of the Internet contains characteristics that encourage creating fantasies of the other person, fantasies that may not survive a live meeting . Fantasy is encouraged by the fact that you often are not looking at the person's reactions—you can't see in their eyes or hear the expression in their voice. The absence of these important visual and auditory cues make it easier for you to be deceived or fool yourself about who this person is. Here are some things to consider when looking for romance online:

- *Computer communication* lacks many cues, such as facial and vocal expression and body language. You will inevitably fill these in, sometimes with inaccurate fantasy images of who you want the other person to be, even when he or she is not deliberately deceptive.
- *On the computer, many people intentionally lie* about some aspect of themselves. Personal photographs sent to others or put on matchmaking profiles are often out of date or altered, and sometimes are even of

another person: When one man finally went to meet an attractive woman with whom he'd been e-mailing through an online dating service, he showed up at her door only to have it opened by her daughter, whom he recognized as the person whose picture was on his date's computer profile!

- *The very nature of computer interaction significantly alters the way communication takes place.* Chatting by e-mail or instant message forces you to take turns. As a result, if the other person is someone who constantly interrupts and dominates a live discussion, you wouldn't know that about him or her. Moreover, because e-mail correspondence allows each person time to formulate his or her thoughts and express them optimally, it can disguise when the person at the other end is socially awkward or too shy to carry on a face-to-face conversation. As much Internet communication is sequential, the opportunity to interrupt is eliminated. Particularly with e-mail correspondence, but even in chat rooms and IM, you can complete your thoughts without the fear of being stopped midstream. In this respect, the Internet makes everyone appear polite.

- *Online anonymity can foster "pseudointimacy,"* leaving you more willing to reveal yourself in ways that you would not normally do in a real-life meeting. The perceived sense of trust and acceptance can lead to the illusion that you know each other very well, whereas this is often false.

- People engaged in online relationships tend to spend more and more time online and less in the real world. This tendency to spend more and more time online can lead you to become increasingly dependent on the cyber relationship for your emotional needs, thereby reducing your practice at socializing in the real world. This developing tendency, plus the perception that being online means you are anonymous and safe, encourages sexualizing online relationships.

- *Correspondence begun in friendship has the potential to turn into erotic dialogue* and then into full-blown cybersex. This may be augmented by the use of Webcams and the telephone. The fantasy and illusion inherent in these situations often leads to unrealistic expectations of what a face-to-face encounter might be.

⌒

AS SO MANY of the stories in this book emphasize, even without overt sexualization, the emotional power and intensity of fantasy relationships can become so great that people married or in committed relationships have left their jobs and families, burned bridges, and traveled long distances to be with someone they've never or barely met, but with whom they're convinced they're in love. Occasionally these relationships do work out, but all too often they are disastrous. In many cases, as with Meghan Daum's experience, a real-life meeting reveals the chasm between fantasy and reality, often leading to a quick ending of the relationship. When cybersex leads to an offline affair, some may be fortunate enough to have a forgiving partner who is willing to take them back. If you are one of those not-so-lucky others you may find yourself losing family, home, and job. Ina, a 38-year-old professional woman who'd been married seventeen years, nearly lost her marriage as a result of a long-distance online relationship that she claims was neither sexual nor romantic, but nonetheless had become all-consuming and compulsive.

THE POWER OF FANTASY: INA'S STORY

It started with a series of e-mails with a man I had never met before but had reason to be in contact with through my work. Elliot is an eloquent writer, as I am; he and I found amusement in that. It escalated. Soon we began to instant message (IM) each other. In this way we became constantly available to each other online throughout the workday. I work from home. He went to his office earlier; I woke up earlier. He stayed at work later; I stayed online later. Then it became weekends, too. While much of our conversation was professional, it became more personal in nature.

His marriage was grim; mine was, too. I viewed our online relationship as a game. We even discussed the infidelity issue. We both justified our continued dialogue. Although there was no discussion of love or romance, or getting together in any permanent way, our contacts progressed and escalated in content and intensity—I was consumed by his e-mails, IM, and phone calls. I was behaving compulsively and I was not able to control it. Eventually I stopped being able to focus on getting anything done at work. I became progressively more isolated and withdrawn. I stopped taking time to be with my kids unless I had to. I was short-tempered and distant from them, because all of my thinking was focused on our intense conversations, and the kids reacted by misbehaving. It was very stressful for the entire family. My emotional distance also hurt my sexual relationship with my husband.

Eventually, I had the opportunity to travel on business to St. Louis, where Elliot lived, and we arranged to meet. I immediately became preoccupied with fantasies about the meeting. The anticipation was very stirring. Although I encouraged my husband, Ben, to stay at home, in the end he came along anyway. Nonetheless, Elliot and I managed to meet. The meeting was a rude awakening; Elliot was nothing like what I had imagined. His humor, his ability to paint wonderful word pictures, his sensitivity—somehow all those qualities I'd liked so much about him—were restricted to his writing. On the computer he had unlimited time to polish his communications. In person, he was inarticulate while at the same time self-righteous and critical. Mark my words: The fantasy is much better!

While we were in St. Louis, Ben became suspicious and I disclosed to him my online relationship with Elliot. Ben just about lost it! He thought I was going to run off with this guy. He asked me if I wanted a divorce. Despite my many reassurances to the contrary, he remained very upset. On the way home, he decided to even the score, by disclosing to me an old affair he'd had. He was obviously trying to hurt me, and was being very cruel. We are now in counseling, dealing with the fundamental relationship issues of secrecy, lying, mistrust, and infidelity. For myself, I am trying to figure out how I got this big emotional hole inside of me that left me so vulnerable to the false thoughts and words of a stranger.

∾

INA'S STORY SHOWS how even in the absence of overt romance or sex on the Internet, a person's search for a fantasy connection can be destructive to both self and family. In therapy, Ina continues to sort out how it is that she was drawn so powerfully and compulsively into her online relationship. After all, she didn't have a history of any Internet romances.

FANTASY VERSUS REALITY

HERE ARE SOME warning signs that you've developed a fantasy relationship on the Internet:

- Reading a new online friend's latest e-mail becomes the highlight of your day.
- You spend hours obsessing about the person and your "conversations."
- You give up time usually spent with friends to stay at home chatting online.
- You think you're in love even though you've never met.

AN OFFLINE MEETING may completely alter your feelings. People already married or in committed relationships who find themselves in the above scenario might consider counseling. Without the reality check that spending time with someone in person provides, it is hard not to endow a new online friend with all those wonderful qualities sought in your ideal fantasy partner. It is a part of being human to project some of our wishes, desires, and even fears onto people we don't know well. But this tendency is enhanced by the pseudointimacy of Internet communication, which can foster soulful sharing of feelings while ignoring the reality that you don't know each other. While this process is fairly normal and under the same circumstances we are all likely to do it, the nature of the online romance intensifies this very human characteristic in ways that can cause harm. To help clarify this, consider the characteristics of healthy romantic love.

ROMANTIC LOVE

IN HIS BOOK, *We: Understanding the Psychology of Romantic Love,* Robert Johnson wrote:

> *Romantic love doesn't just mean loving someone; it means being "in love." When we are "in love," we believe we have found the ultimate meaning of life, revealed in another*

human being. We feel we are finally completed, that we
have found the missing parts of ourselves. Life suddenly
seems to have wholeness, a superhuman intensity that lifts
us high above the ordinary plane of existence. (p.xii)

∾

NO WONDER ROMANTIC love is so powerful and so sought
after! Unfortunately, the circumstances favoring romantic love
also assure that it does not last forever. Romantic love flourishes
when people don't know each other well; when they are unsure
of the other's caring and commitment; when there are barriers
to their encounters, such as physical distance between them
or the need for secrecy; and when there are limits on the time
they spend together. This lack of real knowledge about the other
person guarantees that each will only see the person's desirable
characteristics based on fantasy rather than on reality. When
they get to know each other better, disillusionment is inevitable; only then does the couple have the opportunity to work
on the more challenging tasks of developing real intimacy.

Long-term relationships exhibit a predictable pattern, in
which the early stage of romantic love is followed by a stage
of distancing or disillusionment. During this period many
marriages and committed relationships falter and end. In
successful relationships, this difficult stage is resolved and
followed by the couple coming back together based on a
more realistic understanding and appreciation for the other
person.[11]

Healthy romantic love encourages you to be playful and
vulnerable, and can bring a fresh sense of your self, learned
through seeing your reflection in the eyes of your new partner.
Romance, with or without sex, revitalizes your personal growth;
new relationships encourage fresh insights and self-knowledge.
The beginning stages of a potential love relationship are often

intense and exciting. Most people easily relate to the "rush" of first love and romance, that stuff of songs, greeting cards, and warm memories. Healthy long-term intimacy is characterized by more than romance, intensity, and sex. Intimacy is an experience of knowing and appreciating another over time, of loving who they really are, not what you fantasize them to be. Loving, longer-term relationships develop by using those early exhilarating times as ways to build a bridge toward deeper, longer-term closeness.

Scientists have learned that the brain releases different chemicals at different stages of romantic relationships. That first "rush" of love feeling, which is the experience that love junkies and sex addicts repetitively exploit, has to do with the brain's release of dopamine, a neurochemical that stimulates intense feelings of attraction. Long-term love is characterized by the release of the chemical oxytocin, a much less stimulating drug that produces feelings of satisfaction and contentment. It is now thought that these chemical releases are in place to foster reproduction of the human species. The excitatory intensity of dopamine literally pushes us forward toward mating, sexuality, and the production of offspring. Later in relationships, after the initial excitement has worn off, oxytocin production increases, helping to cement our feelings of attachment, keeping us bonded together to protect and care for our children.

Even with some understanding how the brain rules our emotions, it can be difficult to comprehend how love or sexuality can be exploited or evolve into destructive patterns of addiction and compulsion. Yet for the romance addict and sex addict, romantic love, sexuality, and the closeness these situations offer are experiences often filled with pitfalls, anxiety, and eventual pain. Attempting to love, fearful of being alone or rejected, yet also trapped by fears of being overwhelmed by closeness, romance addicts endlessly long for that "special" relationship, one they can tolerate and depend upon.

If you are a romance or sexual addict, your constant search for someone to love and need you often involves endless intrigue, flirtations, sexual liaisons, and affairs, and leaves in its wake a trail of hurt and destructive consequences. Without support and direction, you will find few options to resolve these painful circumstances other than engaging in even more searching, an escalating cycle of drama, desperation, and loss. Some give up, settling into relationships that are not right for them just to be out of this unhappy cycle. Others continue to struggle and just when they might seemingly be "safe" in a new romantic affair or liaison, instead of becoming comfortable, they grow more unhappy, bored, and fearful and end up pushing perfectly acceptable partners away or starting a new relationship before the current one has ended. Repeatedly running away and/or chasing those who are emotionally unavailable leaves them longing over and over again for another new intense "love" experience. Not understanding the problem or troubling addictive relationship to love and romance, they say, "Maybe next time, the right one will come along."

Unlike psychologically healthy people, who seek partnership and sex to enrich their lives, love addicts search for something outside of themselves (a person, relationship, or experience) to provide the emotional and life stability they themselves lack. Often either hopelessly overcommitted or isolated and deprived of outside stimulation, these people are drawn to find someone "out there" to fill their endless needs. Similar to drug addicts or alcoholics, romance, sex, and love addicts use intensely arousing emotional and sexual experiences to "fix" themselves and remain emotionally stable. As a result, they often make poor partner choices. Compatibility becomes based on "how much you want me," "whether or not you will ever leave me," or "how intense our sex life is" rather than on whether the other might truly become a peer, friend, and companion.

Addictive relationships are characterized over time by

unhealthy dependency, guilt, and abuse (emotional, physical, or sexual). Convinced of their lack of worth and not feeling truly lovable, romance addicts will use seduction, control, guilt, and manipulation to attract and hold on to romantic partners. At times, despairing of this cycle of unhappy affairs, broken relationships, and sexual liaisons, some romance addicts may have "swearing off" periods (like the bulimic or anorexic cycles of overeaters), believing that remaining alone or "just having sex with no love" will solve the problem. Those same problems of intimacy and fear reappear when, tired of being alone, the romance addict reenters the playing field.

∽

THE TWELVE SIGNS OF ROMANCE ADDICTION

1. Do you feel detached or unhappy when in a relationship, yet feeling desperate and alone when out of a relationship? Yes/No
2. Do you avoid sex or relationships for long periods of time to "solve the problem"? Yes/No
3. Are you unable to leave unhealthy relationships despite repeated promises to yourself or others? Yes/No
4. Are you having affairs or intense flirtation and intrigue while already in a relationship? Yes/No
5. Do you return to previously unmanageable or painful relationships despite promises to yourself or others? Yes/No
6. Do you repeatedly mistake sex and romantic intensity for love? Yes/No
7. Do you constantly seek a sexual partner, new romance, or significant other? Yes/No

8. Do you feel incapable of or have difficulty being alone? Yes/No

9. Do you choose partners who are abusive or emotionally unavailable? Yes/No

10. Do you use sex, seduction, and intrigue to "hook" or hold on to a partner? Yes/No

11. Do you use sex or romantic intensity to tolerate difficult experiences or emotions? Yes/No

12. Have you missed out on important family, career, or social experiences in order to maintain a sexual high or romantic relationship? Yes/No

⁓

IF YOU ARE a person addicted to relationship fantasy, these signs or symptoms create an ongoing pattern of emotional instability that inevitably leads to isolation, heartache, and loss. Not everyone who displays any of those behaviors has an addiction problem. At times, almost everyone experiences bad judgment upon encountering a difficult person or seductive situation. However, for romance addicts, heartache and longing become the norm, lived over and over again in one form or another. If these issues apply to you and you are not working toward change or recovery, then you are unlikely to learn from consequences and mistakes. It is much easier to blame your partners and lovers for being "the problem." When the pain of these behaviors and situations becomes greater than the pain and challenges of creating change, recovery begins.

People who are unable to stop their relentless search for a partner may view almost any situation or experience as an opportunity to find that perfect somebody. Upon reflection, you may consider having tried some strategy or another all of your life, attempting to find and keep sexual and romantic partners. One woman put it this way: "I never once went to a party without wondering who I could get a date with or get into bed with. I always dressed for it and looked for it." Whether through revealing dress, flirtatious manner, or seductive talk, the romance addict is continually hunting and searching for that special attention, intensity, and arousal that only the latest tryst or liaison can offer. An important part of the recovery process is recognizing those methods used solely to attract and manipulate others. As addicts begin to consciously cast these aside—using the support of 12-step members, friends, and often therapy—they come to learn their real human worth, lessening the need for superficial, sexualized attention.

CAUGHT ON THE NET WITH A SEX ADDICT

IN THEIR EFFORTS to attract and hold on to a partner, some people become willing to shortcut the path to intimacy by quickly agreeing to engage in cybersex or phone sex. The outcome is often not what the person had hoped for.

Judy's Story

Consider the story of Judy, a 32-year-old divorced woman:

> My husband Ken and I met on the Internet six years ago. We didn't actually engage in cybersex, but quickly developed a phone-sex relationship based on dominance and submission. By the time we met in person six months after first meeting online, we were both in love. I agreed to move halfway across the country to be with him. We married a short time later. Unfortunately, our actual sex life didn't live up to my expectations and was nothing like he promised me on the phone. When he had trouble maintaining an erection, I assumed all the blame, because I was very inexperienced. He was always too tired for real sex, and for a long time I didn't know why. I felt lonely and

paranoid. He told me to initiate sex more, but then when I did, he'd always turn me down. I felt so confused.

One day I accidentally walked in on Ken while he was sitting at the computer. He was masturbating while typing sexual messages to another woman. It turns out that all along my new husband had been having sex with other women through the Internet. Several times I confronted him and threatened to leave. He'd always promise to stop, but he never did. Nonetheless, I would never have left him—I was too terrified to be alone again. I was desperate to keep him, especially after our daughter was born.

Recently my husband "fell in love" with another woman on the Internet. Even before he met her in person, he told me he no longer loved me, and he left to be with her. This has absolutely devastated me. Until I found out about his cybersex activities, I thought this man was the love of my life—my knight in shining armor—despite our sexual problems. Through therapy and by attending Sex and Love Addicts Anonymous meetings, I'm discovering our that relationship was not based on mutual love and respect—only need and desperation.

∾

JUDY IS AN example of a woman who in her quest for romance unknowingly became involved with a sex addict. In her intense desire to please Ken, she willingly had phone sex with him. She assumed that once they developed a real relationship, he wouldn't need or want the cybersex or pornography and would settle into a healthy, loving marriage. Not surprisingly, this didn't happen, and Judy, due to a desperate fear of being alone, enabled Ken's cheating by not following through on her threats to leave. Now, thanks to her therapy, Judy has a clearer understanding of her part in the drama. She wrote:

> *Despite the way we met and how quickly I got attached to him, when I first found Ken chatting up other women online, I made it all his problem and he needed to "fix" it. I had no idea what my part was in the whole situation. Since he left me, I've begun attending a 12-step program and I see a therapist weekly. I'm reading lots of books on addiction, codependency, and love addiction. I now have a better understanding of my role in getting into this relationship in the first place and am working on improving my self-esteem. I hope that if I get into another relationship, I will make a better choice.*

∾

IF YOUR EMOTIONAL needs lead you to look for another person to make you feel whole, and your fear of abandonment makes it difficult for you to trust your own judgment, you are particularly vulnerable to the lure of a cybersex fantasy romance. Many women, like Judy, initially go online to meet a compatible dating partner and agree to participate in online sex to expedite the relationship. Some people, confusing sexual intensity with love, go online specifically seeking sex, believing it will somehow win them love. Unfortunately, when two people meet online and sex quickly becomes the glue to hold them together, it is unlikely that they will be able to convert the relationship successfully to a more traditional one.

MALE ROMANCE ADDICTS

LIKE MANY OF the women described above, men can also get trapped in the illusory nature of online romance. Although most men tend to step deeper into clear-cut porn and overt sexual content than into romantic intensity, there are many cases where the rush and excitement of a new online partner becomes a potent obsession.[12] These connections may start out as a sexual fix or distraction without a relationship, but can develop unexpectedly into more. If you are a male sex, love, or romance addict, you may engage in multiple online relationships at varying stages. You may regularly exchange photos, phone conversations, and sexual chat with several people for purely sexual purposes while also engaging romantically online and offline with several others. Male sex addicts can be like a computer operating system that can keep many "windows" open at one time. When online, you may find yourself conducting multiple sexual and romantic engagements simultaneously, playing each back and forth, usually depending on which is the most emotionally exciting or holds the most promise for sex. Romantic obsession often evolves when the dynamics of an alluring and potentially unavailable partner come into play.

Meeting His Match: Jeffrey's Story

Jeffrey is a 36-year-old professional in a long-term same-sex relationship, with two adopted children:

I nearly lost my lover and our kids because of a fantasy. Until recently, I could regularly be found in the basement "working on the computer." After the family dinner, I'd spend three to four hours, several nights a week, intensely involved in online sex. I kept a daily check-in on my favorite sexual chat rooms, seeing who was there, flirting, hitting on guys, and exchanging photos. I also subscribed to a service where I could order up "models" who would perform "live sex" in whatever way I requested, while I masturbated. Although I never intended to go further than these activities, I felt increasingly drawn to one guy named Spence who did live online porn. At first I became "involved" with him through watching him perform, and over time I would specifically request to see him several times a week.

Over a three-month period, I spent an unbelievable $3,500 on these computer sessions with Spence. During this time, I increasingly withdrew from my partner and family, and found creative ways to lie about where the money was going. Work also became secondary to this cyber affair, as I was checking in with him many times throughout the day. I actually became jealous and afraid he would get "involved" with some other guy online.

❧

LOOKING BACK, JEFFREY acknowledges that the experience became more intense as he began to pursue the "real guy" rather than the fantasy. The object of his intensity became "getting Spence to want me and to tell me who he really was, to put down his work image and let me in." Jeffrey's most intense and arousing moments occurred when Spence finally revealed to him his real name and gave him his personal e-mail address. Jeffrey reports becoming completely hooked at this point, especially when Spence revealed his own tragic life story.

Convinced that he might be "falling in love" with Spence, Jeff requested a live meeting. He made plane and hotel reservations and convincingly lied to his significant other and boss about where he was going and why. It was only in the time he spent talking to their children about why "Daddy would be away for a while" that Jeffrey broke down and realized how out of control he was. At this point, instead of leaving to meet Spence, Jeffrey went out and sought professional help for his problem.

Clearly describing the dynamics that underlie the behaviors of many sex and love addicts, Jeffrey used this online relationship as an emotional power contest: He was trying to get Spence to want him enough to let down his guard and let him in. This became his obsession. The more Spence seemed to count on and need him, alternately pulling away and ignoring him, the more arousing the situation became for Jeffrey, the more "love" he felt and the more he wanted to meet. These issues of dependency, potential abandonment, power, sex, and obsession frequently become intermingled for the male sex and love addict who is desperately seeking consistently and intensely to feel important, wanted, and needed. Unfortunately, these behaviors have much more to do with an adult man acting out unconscious, neglected childhood needs and reenacting childhood emotional traumas, than they have to do with real romantic love or intimacy. In the end, his enacting these unresolved concerns with fantasy partners caused great emotional, personal, and financial losses for him and his family.

WOMEN SEX ADDICTS AND THE COMPUTER

LIKE CHEMICAL DEPENDENCY, sex and romance addiction affect both men and women. Approximately 25 percent of people in sex and love addiction recovery programs are women. Just as with alcoholism, admitting sex addiction is more shameful for women than for men. Even our language reflects this difference: A man who has multiple sexual encounters is known as a "skirt chaser," "ladies' man," "stud," or "Don Juan," while a woman who sleeps with many men is called a "slut," "whore," or "nympho-maniac." It is often more difficult for women to own up to their problem and seek help.

As indicated earlier, studies have shown that men are more interested than women in visual sexual activities (viewing pornographic images and films, voyeurism, and so on.) and in sex with partners who are anonymous or virtual strangers. Women are more likely than men to want romance and relationship as part of their sexual activities.[13] As a result, women constitute the primary readership of the multimillion-dollar soap opera and romance novel industry. Translated to the Internet, men are more likely than women to download and view pornography. Women prefer chat rooms and personal ads, where they can actually "get to know" men. A preliminary study suggests that women cybersex addicts are more likely than men to seek offline sexual meetings as a result of their online sexual activities.[14] The same woman who identifies with the heroine of a romance novel who is swept off her feet by the man of her dreams, now may find herself willing to risk all for the cybersex romance fantasy. Even when having the same goal as a male sex addict—the casual sexual encounter—most female sex addicts are likely to lean toward some type of relationship-oriented sexual encounter as opposed to anonymous sex.

Consider Wendy, a 36-year-old teacher and the wife of a university professor. She reports spending about fifteen hours per week for the past two years in chat rooms. This time had been previously spent on her work or with her husband and three children. Her pattern has been to meet men online and then arrange for an offline encounter with them at hotels or other locations, for the express purpose of having sex. She describes her addiction cycle:

> First I would make up an excuse to leave the house. Then I'd start down my list of potential partners till I found a local guy who was available at the same time I was. I would lie to my spouse and family and go out to meet him. I'd have sex with him and sometimes talk for a few minutes. After the sex, I'd return home as if nothing had happened.

∽

NONETHELESS, HER OWN words reveal that what she really wants is to be loved by an exciting man:

I start to get attached emotionally and it scares the men off;
they just want free sex. I can't seem to have a meaningful
relationship. . . . Usually we just have sex. A few have been
actual relationships, but they never lasted more than a
month . . . I have shut down all my normal emotions and
I just deal with things unrealistically, such as imagining
that some day one of these men will really love me. I shut
out the hurt I feel each time a relationship doesn't work
out. And worse, I repeatedly ignore my family in order to
keep looking.

∾

WENDY'S HUSBAND TED found out about her sexual
acting out eight months earlier when she forgot to turn off her
computer after planning online to meet another man. When Ted
came home shortly after her departure, he read her e-mail correspondence and figured out what was up. Ted confronted Wendy
when she returned. She confessed not only to that meeting, but
also to having had sex with several other men. Wendy cried and
said she knew she had a serious problem, but that the person she
really loved was Ted. She promised to get help, and Ted believed
her but she never did. The only change since then is that she has
been more careful to cover her tracks.

Ted, a quiet, introverted man ten years older than Wendy,
couldn't believe his good luck twelve years earlier when she
agreed to marry him. At his university, Ted is a concerned
teacher who spends long hours at his office doing research
and helping students. Although uncomfortable expressing his
emotions, he cannot imagine life without Wendy, on whom he
is very dependent.

Wendy describes Ted as a caring person who is trying his
best to help her. When asked what is missing in their marriage
and what she is looking for online, Wendy replied:

I love my husband very much and want to stay with him. He loves me to the best of his ability, but for some reason it never seems to be what I need physically, emotionally, or spiritually. There is no passion. I want to be accepted and loved by someone who will be my hero. I know that is not really going to happen, but I keep looking anyway. I haven't bottomed out yet. Why don't I make some real changes? Maybe because I am afraid of being alone, without someone to play with. I love the attention, the letters, the phone calls, etc. Even though I don't crave the sex. I seem to be unable to say no. I place myself in situations that just have a direct path to sex.

∿

WENDY, LIKE MANY sex and love addicts, experienced abuse and emotional abandonment in childhood, the adult effects of which are mostly unseen by her. Often, survivors of childhood abuses (physical, emotional, and/or sexual) confuse sex with love and caring. As children, these people were powerless over what they did or did not get. Many survivors of childhood abuse and abandonment later come to believe that by using sex, flirtation, and seduction they can control over how others feel about them. As adults they tend to use sexualized and romanticized ways of relating to others to affirm their own true value and worth. Their inappropriate behaviors are an attempt to get the consistent love and attention they did not receive as children, without making themselves vulnerable to rejection or loss. As adult survivors and sex addicts themselves, they attempt to use sex to acquire power and a sense of being desired. These dysfunctional attempts to meet deeper emotional needs can be easily stimulated through the sexual stories, pictures, and requests that litter the Internet.

The availability and convenience of Internet connections

can provide a nearly instantaneous means of feeling connected and desired, but at a very high cost. Internet romance keeps addicts searching for love and validation, but often find only more pain and sometimes danger.

Although women usually favor relational activities over straight pornography, some women cybersex users do get hooked on visual images. Yvonne is single and 29 years old, and spends several hours a week online viewing hard-core pornographic photos including those showing sadomasochistic (S&M) activities. Yvonne says:

> *The material that is written for women is usually in the "love addiction" realm and not straight sex addiction. There are women out there like myself who are aroused visually like men and have some characteristics that more closely follow a typical male sex addiction. I don't have sex to appease the man in my life, or get his love; I have sex for the rush of orgasm, for the high, for the medication.*

∽

COMPARED WITH MEN, women cybersex and romance addicts face additional challenges when they seek help because of

- Increased shame about their activities
- Less societal acceptance of women's sexual (and cyber-sexual) behaviors
- Fewer sexual issue 12-step and support group meetings where women feel comfortable
- Lack of knowledge by therapists about cybersex in general, and about women's sexual acting out behaviors in particular

Most of us have enjoyed fantasy in films and books that have enriched our lives. But fantasy is also an important aspect of porn and sex addiction. Looking at pornographic images evokes fantasies in the user's brain that allow him to play out an imagined story in which he may be an active participant, or in which other characters play out scenarios imagined by him. These fantasies are sexually arousing and are often developed during masturbation.

This chapter has described how male and female porn and sex addicts differ. For most women, and for some men, the fantasies may be of romance rather than raw sex. In this chapter you have seen how fantasy and romance can be destructive to the person and to the partner. You have also seen the role of fantasy on the computer and how the desire for romance can hook people on the Net who might otherwise not have gotten into trouble.

In the next chapter you will learn what it's like to be in a relationship with a porn or sex addict. We will explain how to recognize if porn and cybersex are a problem in your relationship, what can happen to the couple's sexual relationship when the partner becomes entangled in the Web, why it's common for the spouse or partner to consider online sex as "cheating," and how cybersex and porn addiction can impact multiple aspects of the couple relationship.

CHAPTER 5

The Porn Widow(er)

My husband has always enjoyed looking at porno. When we were first married he just seemed to be into collecting magazines and videos, which I didn't mind too much as long as he kept it out of the reach of our kids and didn't bring it into our sex life. But as time has gone on, and especially with the Internet, many nights I wake up to find him searching porn sites on the Web and staying up real late masturbating. We have had several fights about this, since I'm in total disagreement with his behavior. A while back I asked him to take one of your online tests that encouraged him to consider counseling or a 12-step approach for sex addiction. He says that the only problem with his porn use is that I have a problem with it and just gets mad at me whenever I bring this up. It's not to the point where it interferes with his work and he always comes home on time and basically he's a good husband and father, but I often feel like he likes the porn more than me and that hurts.

I've been married for four years to an Internet pornaholic, and each time I catch him he has a justification as to why he lied to me. He always says he hasn't done it in a long time but how do I know? Not only that, but he says it's my fault for walking in on him, that he deserves his "me time." I feel powerless to influence his behavior and uncertain about what I should do.

When our relationship got serious, Jon and I agreed that we weren't going to act like some of the other gay couples we knew. We promised each other to be honest and to have integrity around our sex life. When I committed to him it never occurred to me that our definitions of fidelity and respect would differ. While I don't want to believe that he is out there having sex with other men, my trust has been so shredded by his constant online cruising and masturbation to porn that I have trouble holding on to the love he says he feels for me. If he loves me so much, why is he online until three in the morning looking at porn? Why can't he acknowledge the hurt I feel and make me more important than the pictures he spends so much time with? I have always said that I would never stay with a cheater, but what if he really is a porn or sex addict, what do I do then?

I need help with my boyfriend. Since I moved in with him I notice that he keeps porn out everywhere and looks at it almost every night. He says it's a guy thing, because guys are very visual and like to look and watch. He says it is good for us because it keeps him from wanting to stray. Maybe because I am a woman I really can't understand this, I don't know. What I need is to figure out is, how do I get information to help me understand what is really going on here? It has caused a lot of heartache, suspicion, and I am starting to doubt the things he tells me. It's like some kind of paranoid state for me now. If you can help direct me to where to begin to understand what, if anything, I'm dealing with I would be so grateful.

❧

MANY PEOPLE WHO abuse pornography have willing sex partners at home, loving people, who want not only a sexual relationship, but quality time, intimacy, and emotional attention. They want what anyone wants—to feel valued, desired, and connected. The effect that pornography abuse or addiction has on the partner of the abuser is the focus of this chapter. The stories above are just a small sample of the hundreds of e-mails we receive monthly from confused and angry spouses searching for answers to questions like these:

- When do pornography, cybersex, and cyber romance cross the line and violate the integrity of a committed relationship?
- When does looking or chatting become cheating?

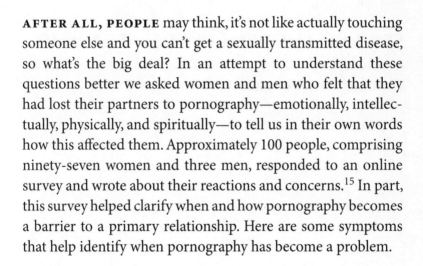

AFTER ALL, PEOPLE may think, it's not like actually touching someone else and you can't get a sexually transmitted disease, so what's the big deal? In an attempt to understand these questions better we asked women and men who felt that they had lost their partners to pornography—emotionally, intellectually, physically, and spiritually—to tell us in their own words how this affected them. Approximately 100 people, comprising ninety-seven women and three men, responded to an online survey and wrote about their reactions and concerns.[15] In part, this survey helped clarify when and how pornography becomes a barrier to a primary relationship. Here are some symptoms that help identify when pornography has become a problem.

Porn use is a problem in your relationship if:

- Your partner is consistently more involved with pornographic pictures, movies, or online sexual interactions than in being physically intimate and sexual with you.
- He or she doesn't want to talk about or consider

changing their porn or Internet sexual involvement no matter how upsetting the issue seems to be to you.

- His or her consistent reaction to your concern about their porn use or online chatting is anger, denial, blaming, or defensiveness.
- Your partner lies to you about his or her porn use or keeping sexual secrets from you.
- He or she makes promises to you about addressing or changing the sexual behaviors but doesn't keep them.

∽

IF ANY OF these symptoms are present in a relationship, then there are bound to be significant negative consequences for that relationship.

SEX AND THE PRIMARY RELATIONSHIP

CONSIDER ELENA, 38 years old, who is in the process of divorcing her husband after a fifteen-year marriage:

I knew my husband was masturbating all the time, but I thought it was my fault, that I just wasn't attractive enough for him. When I finally found the stacks and stacks of pornography magazines and videos hidden in his office, as well as images of women stored on his computer, everything made sense. I had been in denial about how much I knew and how much my life was out of control. I feel very used and violated because of this behavior, and trust is gone.

My husband does not believe he has a problem. He feels it's no big deal since he claims he is being faithful to me. He thinks all he needs is a more accepting wife.

∾

WITHOUT FULLY UNDERSTANDING how the intensity of the porn can affect some people, it would be easy to assume that someone's compulsive porn use simply means they are not getting enough "good sex" at home. This assumption makes it harder for most significant others to reach out for help to family or friends fearing that they will be blamed or judged for "not keeping him [or her] satisfied." As painful as it is for the person whose sexual intimacy has been left behind in the wake of their partner's porn use, it can be just as difficult for those who continue having sex together.

For example, Alexis, thirty-one, who has been married only a year, wrote:

> *Because I know that my husband spends so much time looking at images of other naked women and masturbating to that, I don't want him to touch me. I feel like leftovers, not first-run as I should be. My self-esteem is damaged beyond belief. To be honest, our sex life has always been pretty incredible—we are not prudes by any means. I just don't understand. How can it be soooo good for both of us, but still not enough for him?*

BUT IS IT REALLY CHEATING?

WITH THE ADVENT of digital video-streaming and the relatively insignificant cost of Webcams, images can be captured and sent, and responses returned, all in real time. As the technology of the Internet has advanced, the experience of cybersex and cyber romance has gone beyond still photos and recorded video into live-action images and on-demand sexual responses, or virtual sex. A spouse's pain and confusion is multiplied if the online porn involves real-time online sex with another person. One distraught woman wrote the following:

My husband is using sexual energy that should be used with me. The person on the other end of that computer is live and is participating in a sexual activity with him. They are doing it together and responding to each other. It is one thing to masturbate to a two-dimensional screen image. But to engage in an interactive sexual encounter means that you are being sexual with another person, and that is cheating.

∾

EXTENSIVE INVOLVEMENT WITH porn by one spouse can harm the entire family. The resulting problems come to affect the partner's feelings, the couple's sexual relationship, and other family members.

EFFECTS ON A PARTNER'S EMOTIONAL STATE

THE PARTNERS SURVEYED described their emotional reactions to these betrayals as ranging from devastation and rage to betrayal and abandonment. They spoke of losing self esteem and of having to grieve the loss of intimacy and trust in their relationships. Two women reported actually becoming physically abusive to their husbands, hitting them and throwing objects at them. Others reported feeling sexually inadequate, unattractive, and "downright ugly." Still others came to doubt their own judgment and sanity. Several women and one man reported planning to leave their relationships, and two women had attempted suicide.

The lies associated with sexual activities were a major cause of distress for the partners. One woman wrote, "The lies he told me concerning his whereabouts, while looking me straight in the eye, have hurt worse than his out-of-control sexual behavior." Despite the porn user's repeated promises to stop, the behavior would continue, often with increased lying and secrecy. With each discovery, trust was further eroded. The partners' self-esteem plummeted, and they felt betrayed and rejected. Some described a predominant helplessness that the porn involvement would not end or crease; others primarily experienced feelings of anger.

A 34-year-old man described how his lover's porn use made him feel:

> *I started blaming myself for what he was doing and felt inadequate—not exciting enough, not adventurous enough, etc. I actually got confused about whether this was something I was making into too big a deal, or did I have hang-ups about sex? How could I trust or believe him when he would continually lie to me even when I caught him in the act? Often he would shame me for being "too prudish." He would try to make me feel guilty and often succeeded.*

∾

A 55-YEAR-OLD WOMAN, married thirty-six years, described her range of feelings:

> *This behavior has left me feeling alone, isolated, rejected, and less than a desired woman. Masturbation hangs a sign on the door that says, "You are not needed, I can take care of myself, thank you very much." I have threatened, manipulated, tried to control, cried, gave him the cold shoulder, yelled, tried to be understanding, and even tried to ignore it.*

❦

ONE PORN ADDICT'S perspective was described by a 29-year-old man, with no previous history of compulsive sexual behaviors, who in the three years following the purchase of a computer became caught up in a rapidly progressive addiction:

> *Emotionally I was in a daze for that whole year of being online. I was occasionally there to support my wife, but I seemed always to be thinking about the next time I could get online, and when my next day off of work would be. Sometimes my wife would ask me to pick her up for lunch, and I'd get angry, lying about errands I had to do, so I could stay home and surf the Net. Our relationship became significantly strained. We'd go months without having sex. My wife said she felt extremely alone during that period.*

IS VIRTUAL OR REAL SEX BETTER?

KNOWING THAT THE porn abuser's head is full of newly minted sexual images and fantasies, many can't help but compare themselves to that fantasy person in terms of appearance, desirability, and sexual repertoire. Both porn abusers and partners make such comparisons. Partners feel that they are competing with the magazine, DVD, or computer images. "If only I was perfect like his porn women, then he would want the real thing and love me.""How can I compete with hundreds of anonymous women who now share our bed?" "What am I supposed to do? I am never going to look like the 28-year-old models he looks at all the time." The result is often confusion: on the one hand, a desire to emulate and be as desirable as the porn image; on the other, revulsion at the lack of intimacy and objectified nature of the sex. Survey respondents reported vacillating between these two polarities.

A 38-year-old woman, divorcing after a fifteen-year marriage, confided:

I thought I was not good enough because I did not look like the girls in the pictures. I thought that if I dressed and looked good it would keep him interested. Then I'd give up on competing with his masturbating and not want to have sex with him at all.

∽

ONE GAY MAN put it this way:

We used to always kid about the guys with the perfect bodies we saw at the gym, knowing that what they offered really wasn't anything as good as what we had together. But now that I find him spending night after night on the Internet, I can't help but wonder if that isn't what he wanted all along. Me for empathy and companionship, but them for sex!

∽

INDEED, MANY CYBERPORN addicts do come to prefer virtual sex with fantasy images rather than real-life sex with their partners, so the partner's fears and concerns are justified. A 58-year-old man wrote:

My sex life has always been one of fantasy. After being on the Net and using porn, normal sex with my wife became totally unfulfilling and I no longer felt closeness or intimacy with her.

◦

ACCORDING TO A 45-year-old man,

> *I was so into all the new, physically fit, good-looking women online that I spent less sexual time with my wife and wasn't as turned on by her. What I saw so often became what I wanted to have.*

EFFECT ON THE SEXUAL RELATIONSHIP

TWO THIRDS OF survey respondents described having sexual problems. Often the problems resulted from decreased interest by the porn user in having sex together. In others it was the primarily the partner who lost interest, though in some cases both partners were less interested in sex with each other. Overall, in only 30 percent of the relationships were both members of the couple still interested in sex with each other. Three of the ninety-seven women respondents reported having had extramarital affairs or encounters, either to shore up their own self-esteem or to attempt revenge on their spouses. One of them, a 35-year-old nurse who'd been married eleven years, wrote:

> *We had almost no sex life at all. I was tired of carrying the entire burden of trying to make our relationship work. It got so bad at one point that I began to believe my marriage was over. I started looking around for someone to talk to online. One day in the hospital I ran into a man I'd had a crush on many years before, when I was a nursing student. He had recently moved back to our community after getting a divorce. We went to the cafeteria for coffee, had several other meetings, and eventually I had a one-night stand with him. My husband was so wrapped up in his cybersex that he never even noticed that emotionally I was somewhere else.*

∽

A 34-YEAR-OLD WOMAN, who had learned of her husband's intense online sexual involvement only weeks earlier, described the effects on the couple's sexual relationship:

> *I realize now that many of the things he most liked and requested when we made love were recreations of downloaded images. He is no longer able to be intimate. He objectifies me, other women, and girls on the streets. When we go out it's like his head is on a swivel, staring at every woman that goes by. When we're together in bed, he fantasizes about the women he's seen online and imagines that he's having sex with one of them. I know he does; I can feel it. I have been humiliated, used, betrayed, lied to, and misled. It's almost impossible to let him touch me without feeling really yucky. I tried to continue being sexual with him initially. In fact, I tried being "more" sexual, to compete better with the porn girls, but I couldn't do it. Now we've stopped having sex altogether.*

WHEN THE PORN USER LOSES INTEREST IN INTIMATE SEX

IN ONE THIRD of the survey cases the pornography abuser was no longer interested in sex with his or her significant other. The willing partner reported getting consistent excuses like, "I'm not in the mood," "too tired," "working too hard," "the children might hear," "my back hurts too much," or else he or she would admit to having already had an orgasm that day and not want sex. Even when there was sex, the porn abuser seemed more distant, emotionally detached, or interested only in their own pleasure. The partner ended up doing most or all of the initiating, either to get her or his own needs met, or in a hopeful attempt to get the porn use to decrease. Partners already feeling hurt, angry, sexually rejected, and inadequate reported also being blamed for the couple's sexual problems. In some cases they just went along with sexual activities, even those which they found objectionable to avoid being blamed for being "boring" or "not sexy."

WHEN THE PARTNER ALONE LOSES INTEREST IN COUPLE SEX

SOME PARTNERS FELT so repelled and disgusted by the porn user or cybersex addict that they no longer wanted to have sex at all. Others could not tolerate the ongoing sense of detachment and lack of emotional connection during sex. Some lost sexual interest because they were angry that the porn problem was being denied. Others felt angry, repelled, used, objectified, or "like a prostitute" because of pressure or requests for them to dress in certain ways or perform new sexual acts. In 40 percent of the relationships surveyed, the partners were aware that the cybersex abuser had also had offline sexual affairs. Some of the significant others subsequently avoided sex with the addict out of fear of catching a disease or because a sexually addicted partner had already caught a disease.

A 44-year-old accountant, married twenty-six years to a female sex addict who was his childhood sweetheart, is still in the relationship. He is aware that his wife continues to be involved in cybersex with other men. He has had some therapy but is still working through his anger and depression. He wrote:

At first we had sex more than ever, as I desperately tried to prove myself; then sex with her made me sick. I get strong pictures of what she did and lusted after, and then I get repelled and feel bad. I used to see sex as a very intimate, loving thing. We always had a lot of sex and I felt we were intimate. Since I found out my wife was not on the same page, I can't be intimate or vulnerable—sex is now more recreational or just out of need.

∽

A 49-YEAR-OLD WOMAN, married for nine years to her second husband, describes how initially they had a frequent and enjoyable sexual relationship, but for the past three years sex has been infrequent and perfunctory. She described her dissatisfaction:

> *Sometimes I would "take sex" from him because I felt he owed me that much. But basically any sex that occurred was unsatisfying and left me feeling angry, unwanted, unattractive, and used. Now I don't feel anything when we are sexual. I can no longer reach an orgasm with him. I'm always afraid that any sexual attention he gives me is because he's been viewing cyberporn or talking sexual with someone online. It makes it hard to just enjoy the here and now with him.*

∽

SOME BECAME FRUSTRATED when their male partners justified their intense cybersex involvement as to be "typical of any normal, healthy male." Frustration often turned to anger, and anger led to a loss of interest in the couple's sexual relationship.

DOES MORE REAL-LIFE SEX HELP?

IT IS STILL a common notion that someone who fears a man's "roving eye" while he is out of town should provide him with a night of lovemaking before departure. The mistaken belief is that the good sex at home will somehow keep him from straying while away. In reality, the allure of illicit sex with an unfamiliar partner can survive even abundant sex at home with a willing but familiar mate. This same faulty logic is applied by many partners already aware of the cybersex user's involvement with Internet sex. Some partners either increase the frequency of sexual activities with the cybersex user, or else agree to participate in sexual activities with which they may be uncomfortable or find offensive.

A 39-year-old woman, married eight years but now divorced, wrote the following:

> I tried to initiate a variety of things I saw in Hustler. I feel ashamed about what I've suggested, which I thought would change his behavior. I have to remind myself every day that that wasn't my normal behavior. I am trying to forgive myself. It's extremely difficult.

∽

SOME PARTNERS EVEN go so far as to join the user in cybersex activities. Like the following 34-year-old woman, who has been married for fourteen years, they usually learn that their involvement in these activities does not prevent the porn addict from continuing to engage in compulsive masturbation with porn or even online sex with other people.

> My husband is a minister who was stationed overseas for a year. We chatted daily, but never sexually. One day he admitted to me that he'd been involved in cybersex activities with other women online. He said it had nothing to do with us and that it didn't affect his feelings for me. I felt cheated. Why wouldn't he ask me to have cybersex? I guessed it was because he thought I was too old-fashioned, so I told him I was willing to try it with him. I wasn't

comfortable with this, but I thought I could "rescue" him. We began a long-distance online sexual relationship. But much to my horror, he never quit with the anonymous partners. Instead he lumped me together with all the online whores. When he returned, he continued his cybersex even though we were reunited. We're still together, but his online activities have really come between us.

∽

ATTEMPTS TO SOLVE the porn problem by providing more real-life sex are usually ineffective and are mostly short-lived. It's common for those who participated in activities with which they were uncomfortable to feel shame and anger later. Trying to control a sex addict's behavior and get his or her attention with another sexual act is usually unsuccessful.

WHAT'S THE BIG DEAL ABOUT ONLINE SEX?

SOME COMPULSIVE PORNOGRAPHY users never leave the isolation of their sexual fantasy worlds; others use Internet porn as a gateway to live sexual encounters with other people. To help readers understand why marriages and long-term relationships break up even though pornography doesn't involve skin-to-skin contact, we asked people who experienced this situation to present their viewpoint in the survey. Here are the most common reasons for such break-ups:

- a concern about escalation of the behaviors
- the belief that a cybersex affair is still cheating
- the effect on the partner's self-esteem
- the effect on the marriage and children
- being unable to trust again

༄

THE FIRST THREE reasons will be examined in more detail here Chapter Six will address the impact of an adult's use of pornography on children.

Concern about Escalation

ONE ISSUE COMMON to those who use pleasure-seeking behavior for emotional escape is their *increasing tolerance* to the mood-altering effects of the behavior. In other words, over time either the person has to do more and more of the same behavior to get the same level of excitement, or they have to get into increasingly more intense experiences to produce the desired effect. Online viewing, for example, which may begin as harmless recreation, can become an all-consuming activity, taking the user away from family and work. It can also lead to offline sexual encounters with those met online or even a need for real-life sexual activities that aren't computer related. According to our survey respondents, 40 percent of the cybersex addicts had also engaged in offline sexual activities. This surely is an underestimate, since it is likely that not all partners were aware of such behaviors.

Some cyberporn abusers do describe a progression of their addiction. A 32-year-old man with a prior history of compulsive sexual behaviors wrote:

> Online pornography really accelerated my addiction. It went from just pornographic magazines and movies to spending hours on end on the computer looking at images, and finally to many hours chatting with anyone who would engage in sexual "talk" with me. It took only three months to go from simple e-mail correspondence to all this. Had my wife not found a porn disk in my disk drive and confronted me, it would have only been a

matter of time before I started to meet women in person. Considering my shyness and preference of fantasy over being with real women, meeting a live woman would have been a big step!

∽

DESCRIBING THE ACTIVITIES of her husband, whose business often took him away from home, a 41-year-old woman, formerly married five years, related:

My husband's compulsive sexual activities quickly progressed. He first got into print pornography, then real-time cybersex that led to phone sex. Next he answered personals and placed his own ads when out of town. This evolved into his placing an ad in porno sites for group sex and discreet affairs. He's had multiple partners. He deceives women by telling them that he's single and lives in the town he's due to work in.

∽

IN OTHER CASES, even when no live sexual encounters occurred with people the addict met online, the sexual activity did trigger other addictive behaviors. One gay man wrote that since being online, his partner had begun to go out and have anonymous sex. Others wrote that their partners had begun new activities such as visits to sexual massage parlors, hiring prostitutes, having a first affair, or additional affairs.

On the Internet it is possible to find groups of people who are interested in all kinds of unusual or even deviant sexual practices. Interacting with these people helps to desensitize the user and "normalizes" these activities. Some cyberporn users eventually blame their partners for their relationship problems, citing their unwillingness to engage in these behaviors. Even if the viewers' activity never goes beyond traditional pornography, prolonged cyberporn use can negatively affect the viewer, as this 30-year-old single man discovered about himself:

> *Throughout the last couple of years, the more porn I've viewed, the less sensitive I am to porn that I used to find offensive. Now I get turned on by some of it (anal sex, women urinating, etc.). The sheer quantity of porn on the Net has done this. It's so easy to click on these things out of curiosity in the privacy of your own home. The more you view, the less sensitized you become. With magazines and video I used to be only into soft-core porn showing the beauty of the female form. Now I'm into explicit hard-core.*

CYBERSEX IS STILL CHEATING

TO THE SURVEY respondents who considered their partner's extensive porn involvement to be the same as adultery, the lying and emotional unavailability of their partner felt the same as a real affair would. Many felt that the lies, which are often the most painful part of a real-life affair, were just as excruciating with someone involved with porn. They felt betrayed, devalued, deceived, "less than," and abandoned—the same as with a real affair. They mourned the loss of the sexual intimacy they previously had. One woman wrote, "I may not be getting a disease from him, but I'm not getting anything else either!" In real-life, it is hard for a loving partner to compete with the excitement of an affair. Similarly, with porn and family fantasy affairs, partners are competing with idealized, fantasy others who are always available, make no demands, and are willing to do whatever the user wants. The pain is even greater if the cybersex addict is having real-time online sex with another person. Most agreed that a partner's extensive involvement with pornography *is definitely being unfaithful* and real-time online sex, *a violation of monogamy.*

Finally, many survey respondents complained that pornography took their spouse away from the relationship itself. The resulting emotional detachment was viewed as a real loss. A 39-year-old woman, married fourteen years, explained:

> *He did have affairs, although not physically. He had affairs of the mind and that to me is as much a violation as if he actually had a physical affair with someone. According to my religious beliefs, he committed adultery just the same as if he had another real partner. Moreover, in one sense I feel that having an affair of the mind is worse than having an actual partner. My husband can, at any time, have an "affair" without leaving the house or seeing another human being.*

∾

THE 40 PERCENT of the partners who knew about an actual prior extramarital sexual encounter were able to compare how they felt about their partner's pornography activities versus how they felt about their affairs. Several experienced the same hurt. A 38-year-old woman, married eighteen years, shared:

> *They should try it for themselves one time, and see how it feels to be less important to their partner than a picture on a computer screen! They should see what it feels like to lie in bed and know their partner is on the computer and what he is doing with it. It's not going to do much for their self-esteem. My husband has actually cheated on me with a real partner, and it feels no different! The online "safe" cheating feels to me just as dirty and filthy as does the "real-life" cheating.*

PARTNER'S SELF-ESTEEM

COMPULSIVE PORN ABUSE by one partner in a relationship taps into the other's deepest insecurities about his or her ability to measure up. The need to compete with fantasy images and cyberporn pressures can leave partners feeling pressured into unwanted sexual activities. "Fantasy sex leaves practically nothing to be desired when compared with the all-too-human and flawed spouse," explained one woman. Another woman wondered: "When he closes his eyes when we are together, what is he thinking of? The babe in the movie? Is he happy with my body? Is he grossed out?"

Even the best-adjusted person is likely to feel bad when repeatedly seeing someone they love preferring solitary sex with a magazine or video image to flesh-and-blood lovemaking. A 37-year-old woman, married seventeen years, explained:

> *True, you don't have the risk of the diseases, but it is still an emotional thing. It's hard to think that he wants to do it without the actual human touch of another—how can it be better for him? Especially since he has to do all the work himself! Even when he is having sex with me, he's not really there emotionally. I know he is thinking about and picturing the "others," what he would be saying to them, etc. In reality, he is getting off on something that has nothing to do with me. It really hurts my self-esteem, and I never had very good self-esteem to begin with.*

∽

AS WE DESCRIBED in this chapter, partners of pleasure seekers and pornography addicts are likely to experience shame, doubt, loss of self-esteem, self-blame, a worsening of their sex life, depression, and anger. They are then likely to embark on a course of action that often includes ongoing detective work, bargaining with the cybersex user, and attempting to control the behavior. Some may leave their relationships, temporarily or permanently. No matter what happens to the relationship, nearly all partners feel violated and should get help and support for themselves. Such help is described in later chapters in this book.

The next chapter will present information on how pornography, especially Internet porn, can affect children and teens, and discuss the resources available to families to deal with this increasing problem.

CHAPTER 6

Teens, Kids, and Pornography

I am a parent of a college boy who is struggling with Internet pornography. I need help in starting to talk with him about this and we both need some clear direction. Who or what group can I go to get help for him and find out how I can help? This has taken his self-esteem down to zero; he says he won't even go out on dates because he feels so embarrassed about what he has been doing in private. I don't really know how to advise him.

I never really understood much about the computer beyond sending e-mails and writing the occasional letter. Last week I was looking at my 15-year-old son's computer while he was at school and much to my horror I found that he had been extensively visiting graphic porn and sex sites. I think he also has a big file of porn images, over 100 pictures, but I haven't been yet able to open that file to see what is inside. What should a parent do in this situation? I don't want to shame my son, but his behavior violates my beliefs and breaks a lot of rules I thought that we had established as a family.

IN MANY HOMES, it is the youngest ones who are the most computer savvy. Kids often know more than their parents do. Now that most homes in the United States have computers, it's no wonder that parents are increasingly concerned about what their children are exposed to on the Internet. Until recently, perhaps the worst thing a parent had to worry about regarding their child's exposure to pornography was a hidden copy of *Playboy* under the mattress or a collection of sexual pictures in a child's clubhouse. Kids may have inadvertently seen sexual or romantic activity between other kids and adults in parks or automobiles, a calendar image in a garage or store, or perhaps they viewed a porn video at a party with other teens. How innocent this all seems now!

While every generation of parents tends to distance themselves from what they were like as kids while anxiously scrutinizing the music, dress, and burgeoning sexuality of their own children, this generation has identifiable reasons for concern. The Internet has brought about a sea change in the access that children have to pornography. This is especially true for those kids who have grown up with the Internet all their lives, as many have their own computers and either deliberately or inadvertently visit sexually oriented Web sites. Some, without seeking it, are the recipients of sexual content on their computers or of sexual invitations from predatory adults.

This chapter will help you:

- Understand the online risks children and teenagers face
- Protect your kids when they're online
- Help kids who are already into cybersex or cyberporn
- Safeguard your children when a parent in the home is a pleasure seeker, porn abuser, or sex addict

THE ONLINE RISKS CHILDREN AND TEENAGERS FACE

IN 2000, 13-YEAR-OLD Justin Berry obtained a free Web camera by joining Earthlink, an Internet Service Provider (ISP). He hooked up the Webcam to his computer, hoping to use it to meet other teens online. But within a few minutes of beaming a live video feed of himself through cyberspace, he was instant-messaged by a man who soon offered Justin fifty dollars to remove his shirt and display his naked chest. Naïve at the time, Justin thought it was an easy way to make big money. This was the beginning of a five-year career of selling images of his body on the Internet and, later, meeting men in person and having sex with them. In addition to exhibiting himself, he eventually began to perform live sex acts online to paying audiences of up to 1,500 people. He netted hundreds of thousands of dollars. He also became addicted to cocaine and marijuana.

At nineteen, after being contacted by a reporter from the *New York Times*, Justin finally decided he'd had enough. He quit using drugs, closed down his Web site, and turned over his files to federal authorities. He agreed to become a witness in a wide-ranging federal investigation of online child pornography. On December 19, 2005, Justin's story was told in an extensive front-page *Times* story. As a result of his disclosures, hundreds of men were arrested. On May 16, 2006, the *New York Times* reported the arrest of one of these men, a 28-year-old computer consultant who had not only lured 13-year-old Justin to his home and molested him, but also facilitated setting up Justin's Web site.

Justin was just one of many young people involved in the burgeoning industry of self-produced child pornography. The technology needed to participate in this lucrative but damaging activity is now inexpensive and widely available.

According to a 2005 *New York Times* report, 14 million U.S. households had Webcams, inexpensive miniature cameras costing less than twenty-five dollars, which easily feed live images through the Internet. Real-time communication through instant messaging (IM) allows customers to rapidly contact young entrepreneurs and innocent teens who are looking only for friendships. Internet telephony now allows phone conversations online, the same as a telephone. Legitimate Web pages and sites used by teens seeking friends are infiltrated by adults, some of whom impersonate teenagers to "make friends" with them, learn about them, and groom them for sex. Online payment sites enable rapid transfer of funds. Additionally, Web sites such as Amazon.com contain the electronic version of department-store wish lists, which makes it easy to send gifts to young people.

There are other less extreme, risks for teens online. One of the most common is making a "friend" online in a teenage chat room but not realizing that the friend is in fact an adult child predator representing himself as a teen. Because this is such a common occurrence, teen chat rooms are now heavily infiltrated with FBI and other officials hoping to trap a predatory adult and shut down his or her activities. Almost on a daily basis, newspapers report accounts of arrests of adults who meet teens for sex.

In 1999 and 2000 a survey was conducted of a random sample of 1,500 youth ages ten through seventeen who were regular Internet users. The results, published in 2001, showed that 19 percent of these children had been the targets of unwanted sexual solicitation during the previous year. Girls, older teens, troubled youth, frequent Internet users, chat room participants, and those who communicated online with strangers were at significantly greater risk. Twenty-five percent of the solicited youth reported high levels of distress after solicitation incidents. The study authors concluded, "Health care professionals, educators, and parents should be prepared to educate youth about how to respond to online sexual solicitations, including encouraging youth to disclose and report such encounters and talk about them."[16]

Many young Internet users give out information online that makes them vulnerable to exploitation by sexual predators. The National Center for Missing and Exploited Children (www.missingkids.com) reported on a survey of 1,500 teens, ages twelve to seventeen, who used the internet between 1999 and 2000. Twenty-one percent of them posted their e-mail addresses, 11 percent posted personal information such as their age or location, 8 percent admitted having deliberately visited X-rated Web sites, 7 percent had posted a photo of themselves, and 4 percent had talked about sex online with someone they'd never met. If this survey were repeated now, when the percent of homes that have internet access is so much greater than 2000, then surely the figures would be much higher.

In 2005, *Dateline NBC* began a series of nationally televised sting operations where adults posing as young kids (12 to14 years old) went into teen chat rooms and pretended to be kids whose parents were out of town. In city after city around the country, adult men—from college students and physicians, to grandfathers and teachers, single and married—showed up seeking to have sex with a minor, generally under the guise of wanting to make friends. In one such California case, more than fifty men presented themselves in a 48-hour period to find the young teen they had "met" online for sex. And lest there be any doubt as to their intent, not only did many of these men send photos of their genitals online to these "kids" and write intimate sexual details to them, but many brought condoms, lubricants, and liquor to share with their potential young partners.

HOW TO PROTECT YOUR KIDS WHEN THEY ARE ONLINE

HERE ARE SOME suggestions to help prevent your children from becoming hooked on the Net, and to protect your children from cybersex predators:

- Limit computer privacy by placing any computer with Internet access in an area of the house where the child's computer use can be easily monitored.

- Monitor your child's Internet use by checking the computer's bookmarks, history of Web sites accessed, and caches. Consider computer software such as Disk Tracy (www.disktracy.com) that provides a list of every online site accessed by the computer on which it is installed.

- Install blocking software such as CyberPatrol (www. cyberpatrol.com), Net Nanny (www.NetNanny.com), or Cybersitter (www.cybersitter.com), which will deny access to sexually inappropriate sites, including instant messaging. Other brands of Internet filtering software include Norton Internet Security, McAfee Privacy Service, We-Blocker, ContentBarrier for Mac, and SurfControl.

- Consider using an Internet Service Provider (ISP) that is "family oriented," which blocks any sexually inappropriate material from even reaching your computer. You can ask your provider about parental controls.

- Advise your child *never to reveal to anyone* their real name, address, or phone number, nor provide any information that will make it easy to locate them (such as name of school), without your permission.

- Let children and teens know that *it is never acceptable to go out to meet someone whom they met online.* Should they wish to do so, such a meeting must be parentally supervised.

- Talk with your children about their Internet activities. Encourage your children to inform you of any online experiences or conversations that make them uncomfortable. If you believe your child is being sexually exploited or that someone is attempting to exploit him or her, consider this to be a crime and report it to the police or FBI.

- Learn more about the Internet, so you can better monitor your child's activities. Many organizations offer workshops on how to use computers and the Internet.

- A good place to file a report is the CyberTipLine (www. cybertipline.com or 1-800-843-5678). According to the CyberTipLine, between January and December 2004 they received 106,119 reports of child pornography, 559 reports of child prostitution, 2,605 reports of online enticement of children for sex acts, 248 reports of child sex tourism, 533 cases of unsolicited obscene material sent to a child, and 487 misleading domain names. These numbers have been growing every year since this agency was founded in 1998, and in 2004 were approximately thirty-two times greater than the figures for 1998.

HELPING KIDS WHO ARE ALREADY INTO CYBERPORN OR CYBERSEX

WE'VE ALREADY DISCUSSED how to help cyberproof your child from someone on the outside. But what about if you discover that your daughter is already engaged in online sexual talk with unknown persons on the Net? Or your son is viewing and downloading pornography? At first it may not be clear how serious a problem this is. Is this an occasional activity, or are they spending hours online? Children who have discovered cybersex are likely to keep their activities secret from the parents. Therefore, in addition to asking them directly about their computer activities, review what is happening in their lives:

- Has their school performance dropped or are they maintaining their grades?
- Are they still engaging in their usual after-school sports and social activities, or have they dropped out?
- Is their mood the same as usual, or have they become moody, depressed, or anxious?
- Have they become more secretive about how they spend their time and where?

∾

IF YOU DO *not find any worrisome signs* but still suspect your child, then begin by instituting some of the measures discussed earlier in this chapter, such as moving the child's home computer to a public place, having a family-friendly ISP, installing blocking software, and posting your family computer rules on or near the computer itself. However, because your child will of course continue to have access to computers in other locations, such as the school, library, Internet cafes, and friends' homes, limiting cyberporn access in the home is only the first step.

You will need to have some calm discussions with your child, emphasizing the need to respect people and their bodies. For example, "How would you feel if that picture were of your sister or of Mom?" Also talk about the risks of the Internet, including the reality that people are not always honest and they may misrepresent themselves in online conversations. For example, an adult may pose as a child. Once you feel you have resolved the present problem, don't become complacent about your children's Internet use. You will need to continue to monitor their online activities. Also, be open to discussing any inappropriate content they find online, and have an ongoing dialogue with them.

If your child is already experiencing negative consequences, such as poor school performance, isolation, and mood changes, and you know or believe this is related to their online activities, then you should seek professional help, especially from a counselor who understands teens and is familiar with computer-related problems (see the Resources section at the end of this book).

⌒

YOU CAN DISCUSS porn and cybersex in much the same way you might talk to kids about drinking, gambling, or driving, pointing out the difference between adult and teen privileges. Those committed to having a "porn-free" home also need to be able to honestly talk to their kids about their beliefs and expectations of each other as a family. This kind of open, age-appropriate conversation can be integrated into any general discussion about sexual health, intimacy, and growing up.

WHEN AN ADULT IN THE FAMILY IS A PLEASURE SEEKER, PORN ABUSER, OR SEX ADDICT

OFTEN, PORN ACTIVITIES take time away from being a parent. Abusers often go through the motions of parenting without the emotional investment required to help children feel bonded and attached. Spouses may also become less available for parenting due to their preoccupation with their significant other's sexual activities. In cases where parents divorce, the children lose the presence of a parent in the home. Even in relationships that remain intact, children often witness arguments, conflict, and stress in the home.

In some cases, the children actually come upon and view the pornography or witness a parent masturbating at the computer. Some children find pornography left on the computer, walk in when the cybersex abuser is checking someone out in a chat room, overhear a parent having phone sex, or observe interactive online sex. Several mothers were worried because their husbands surfed the Net while supposedly babysitting young children. Sometimes these children were inadvertently exposed to the pornography and masturbation. In some families, teenage children began viewing online pornography themselves.

The following letter is typical of a parent whose partner abuses porn in the home:

I am married to a man who has had stacks of porn magazines in our home and spent many hours a week looking at naked women online. I am concerned about the possibility that my kids will come in contact with these images or actually see him in his online sexual activities.

∾

IF AN ADULT in the home is heavily involved with porn, it is unrealistic to expect that children and teenagers in the home will not learn about this, want to find out more about it, and access online sexual material themselves. If parents have a problem with porn or sexuality, they have to deal with it and bring healing to it before they will be very effective with their children. The first step to having a healthy family is for the parents to deal with their own problems.

It's very important to be honest with children in an age-appropriate manner. If they ask questions about your or another adult's off- or online pornography behavior, be prepared in advance with how you want to handle it. If moderate porn use is acceptable to you and your spouse, there are ways of talking to kids about the difference in what is appropriate for adults and children.

This is also a good time to talk with your children about all other forms of pornography: magazines, videos, and cable television films. Relate to them that pornographic images treat the subject of the picture as an object, and that repeated viewing can lead to objectifying women, for example, in general. It is also a good time to go over the house rules regarding pornography, and to check in on your adjustable television and Internet parental controls. Your goal is to instill healthy values in your

PROTECTING CHILDREN FROM A PARENT'S PORN USE.

Although my husband says he's in recovery from his sex addiction, I believe he is continuing to visit inappropriate Web sites when our sons are around. My question is this—should I attempt to protect my children from their father's behavior by limiting their access to him, or let them spend time with their father unsupervised and deal with the consequences?
    —A married woman whose husband is a sex addict

In a home where porn use by one adult is a problem, the most pressing concern of the other parent is likely to be how to protect the children in the home. If the porn abuser is a sex addict, whether or not he is in recovery from his addiction, the other parent has good reason for concern about preventing the next generation from having similar problems. If partners are separated or divorced, the question arises of whether it is safe for the children to spend time in the home of the porn-using parent or even to have contact with him.

The court process is traumatic for children, which on its own can create a great deal of stress for a child. Whether married to a user of porn, or separated or divorced from a person with an addiction, you should consult an attorney if you wish to better understand your rights and the rights of your children.

If you wish to work through this situation with the other parent, a therapist can be very helpful in providing you with healthy coping mechanisms. A therapist may also be able to help you navigate a discussion with your partner about your fears. Remember, the healthier you are, the greater support you will be to your children.

Similarly, children often benefit from discussing their feelings and experiences with a therapist. Even if a child hasn't been exposed to a parent's porn, they are likely aware of the tension in the home.

Regardless of the path you choose, please don't feel that you need to handle this on your own.

children, values that will guide them when you are no longer able to directly influence their behavior.

WHEN CHILDREN DISCOVER A PARENT'S PORNOGRAPHY

I live with my parents and discovered about a year ago that my father is a so-called "porn addict." I guess it's been an issue for a long time but heightened by the presence of the Internet. He told my mom at dinner that he was warned about surfing online at work but didn't listen and got fired. I'm seeking assistance and personal counseling to learn how to deal with this situation and how to best deal with my parents. To be honest, what I'm experiencing the most is anger. My folks have been married more than 30 years and may or may not make it past this. I don't even want to deal with my father, I'm angry at my mother for being so weak about the whole situation. In general, I'm just confused.

UPON DISCOVERING A father's cyberporn collection, a mother's online affair, or observing a parent masturbating at the computer, a child experiences a great deal of emotional turmoil. Depending on age, these emotions may include:

- Confusion and misunderstanding mixed with interest and arousal
- Shock at the parent's behavior
- Wonder at what this means for his parents' relationship
- Embarrassment at having to face that the parent is a sexual person
- Anger that one parent may be betraying another
- A sense of loss that Mom or Dad is not the idealized person the teen may have thought she or he was
- Fear that the marriage will end and one parent may leave
- A sense of power at holding an important family secret
- Curiosity to learn more about what's available online

WHAT ADVICE CAN we give to kids who find themselves in this situation? Here is what you can tell them:

- Don't deal with this alone.
- Don't keep it to yourself; talk with a trusted adult—a relative, a teacher, a minister, a counselor—about the situation and what to do about it.
- Before assuming it's one parent's fault or the other's, wait until you have more information.
- Adults sometimes look at images or have experiences that are out of the range of what kids do. This doesn't necessarily mean that something is wrong or bad. Discourage them from prying or doing "detective work" to find out more.

❧

CHILDREN WHO HAVE learned private information such as a parent's sexual activities need to hear an explanation from the parents as well as have their feelings validated. The explanation should be age-appropriate.

- Young children ages nine to thirteen want to know: Am I normal? Did someone do something bad by looking at this? What will happen to me if you get divorced?
- Teenagers want to know: What does this mean about your [the parents'] relationship? How could you do this to Mom/Dad/to the family? How does this specifically relate to me? (You've ruined my life!) If you do that, am I going to do it, too?
- Children of all ages want to know that the parents will handle the situation, that these issues will be talked about and worked through, not just left hanging there.
- It is harmful to kids for one parent to attempt an alliance with the child against the other parent, or for either parent to make a child into their confidant. It is amazingly destructive to a child for an angry parent, feeling violated about their spouse's pornographic or sexual involvements outside marriage, to share these issues with a child or teenager who could not possibly have the emotional resources to understand these issues.

❧

FINALLY, IN THIS day and age it is essential that children have helpful, well researched, age-appropriate information about their own human physical and sexual development, childhood crushes, and about the path to adult sexuality. The

IMPORTANT NOTE ON P2P FILE-SHARING:

Blocking software will not help screen out peer-to-peer file-sharing network (P2P) programs that allow you to download materials online directly from someone else's computer onto your own. To block this type of download, you have to find a trustworthy and computer-savvy person to act as your computer's administrator. They then have to put limits on your user account to keep peer-to-peer programs from being installed altogether.

better informed a child is, the less likely it is that seeing an inappropriate image or having a troubling experience is going to produce further harm. Most important, children need to feel that they can discuss sexual issues without the fear of shame or embarrassment. Now, more than ever, kids need to feel that they can talk to a parent about anything.

The following two chapters provide guidelines, plans, and direction that actually work to eliminate destructive patterns of pornography abuse and addiction—provided you do the work.

CHAPTER 7

Doing the Work to Get Well

ONCE YOU ACCEPT the fact that you have a pornography problem, which has not been solved by *making promises, self-will, or self-determination,* you need to consider additional resources and methods of change. To make your life different, you must first honestly acknowledge that a real problem exists and that you need help. There is no other way to start. Even a grudging willingness and superficial understanding is a beginning.

∽

A PLAN FOR CHANGE

THOSE STRUGGLING WITH pornography abuse and Internet sex need help to get better. Porn abusers and sex addicts cannot truly change their behavior by themselves. The very nature of these problems implies a kind of distorted thinking; therefore, the person with the problem needs both the insight and the accountability that only an objective person can provide. Declarations like, "I swear I will never go to X-rated sites again!" or "As long as I live, I will never go into another adult bookstore!" are not enough to keep you out of trouble when you are challenged by temptation and arousal. As you have probably already discovered, mere promises made to yourself and others that "things will change" usually don't amount to much and end up letting everyone down, including yourself.

However, changes will occur if you work toward them.

Here are the first action steps toward change, whether your pornography problems are in the home, office, or on the road:

1. *Find an accountability partner.* This is someone to help you be accountable for the work ahead. This person's job is to simply be available for you to check in with (in person or by phone) regarding the new changes and commitments you are making. Making use of this person's help is an essential step toward healing and should not be dismissed lightly. If no one else is available, in the beginning this role can be filled by a wife, husband, or significant other, but over time it is best to find a more neutral person to help you. Ideally this person would be someone that you do not find sexually attractive and who has struggled with his or her own pornography or sexual problems and found healing through a sexual addiction 12-step program, therapy, or other support group. A clergy member, addiction counselor, or therapist trained in working with sexual addiction can also serve as your accountability partner (see Resources in the back of this book).

    It felt too shameful to turn to my husband for support when I wanted to go online. I just knew that he would end up blaming himself or feeling inadequate no matter how much he wanted to help. It really got better when I found someone to help who wasn't so directly affected by my problem. They were able to be my reality check when I needed someone who could understand and not get angry or hurt.

    While it can feel embarrassing and silly to have to check

in with another person, keep in mind, if you really do have a problem, then you really do need help from others to get well. Asking for help can be humbling, but will greatly increase your chances for success. In the beginning you may find that you need more than one person's help.

2. *Throw out all pornography.* Box up *all* tapes, books, magazines, DVDs, videos, CDs, adult bookstore tokens, and related paraphernalia (lubricants, toys, etc). Take the box to a commercial trash Dumpster at least a mile from your home, drop it in the Dumpster and leave it in there.

3. *Call your accountability partner* to let them know that you have thrown out your porn stash and commit to not buying any more. Promise them that if you feel like buying more porn, you will call them back *prior to doing so.*

4. *Cancel memberships at video rental stores.* Get rid of all membership cards at stores that sell or rent porn. If you must rent films, do so at Blockbuster and other stores that don't offer XXX material and take someone along with you when you go to rent movies.

5. *Stay out of R or unrated movies.* Leave these films to people who don't have a sexual problem. For someone with addictive sexual behaviors, they can reopen the door to problem behavior.

6. *Throw out all porn magazines* and catalogs with strong sexual content, such as lingerie catalogs.

7. *When traveling, call ahead* to see if the accommodations where you will be staying offer adult movies in their rooms. If so, ask if these films can be blocked— they usually can. Ask them to block them for you or if necessary, block them when you get into your room, and then call your accountability partner to let them know you have done so.

8. *Avoid reading any material that contains* advertising for sensual massage or escorts (urban weekly arts magazines, for example).

IF ONLINE PORN AND CYBERSEX IS (A PART OF) YOUR PROBLEM:

1. *Go through your computer files and history* while being monitored by your accountability partner. Delete all downloaded files and old mail with pictures or attachments, often found as GIF or JPEG files. Use the computer's search ability to look for items with the words *sex, porn, photo*, and so on. Delete *all* files with sexual or romantic content—letters, photos, e-mail, sexual jokes, and pornography. The other person is nearby to hold you accountable to the task at hand. That person will ensure that mail is not longingly reread, old photos glanced at, or online relationships reengaged. There is no need to review this stuff; just get rid of it.

2. *Purchase and install blocking software!* Blocking software designed to eliminate access to sexual content and other specific types of sites can be purchased in computer stores or downloaded over the Internet. This software, which will screen out 90 percent of sexual sites is a *must have* for those with cyberporn problems who intend to use the Internet again. Although with enough effort the software can be defeated, it provides time to reflect before logging on to an inappropriate site. It is essential when loading this software *to give the access code to someone else*. Without the access code, it is impossible to remove the blocking software. Some helpful blocking programs are listed in the Resources section of this book. Put the software on *all your computers*, not just the ones you have used for accessing sexual material.

3. *Move your home and work computer.* Porn abusers and sex addicts who live with others should not keep their home computer in an isolated location. Put the home computer in the family or living room. If your office computer screen faces away from people walking by or entering your workstation, move the screen so that others can view what is being accessed.

4. *If you can avoid it, don't travel with a laptop.* If you must use a computer when traveling, commit to using it only in public areas of hotels or airports. Alternately, leave your computer at home and use a hotel business center or local Internet coffee house.

5. *Go online only when someone else is home.* Account-ability is established by having others around. If you live alone, call your accountability partner to let them know when you are going online and check back in with them after you are done. *At work, go online only during work hours.* Don't stay late to work on projects and take on assignments involving Internet use. Avoid being alone in the office.

6. *Change online providers.* Several Internet Service Providers (ISPs) offer access only to sites that their evalu-ation team has deemed are appropriate for children and families. Such providers exclude sexual and violent content and limit viewing to the sites deemed appro-priate for their network. Some of these ISPs are listed in the Resources section at the end of the book.

7. *Go online for e-mail only.* If there is no reason to be online—don't go online. Make a written and verbal commitment to avoid any unplanned online searching or activity. Let others gather information or data if that becomes necessary. Stay out of all chat rooms. Don't instant-message anyone who isn't a family member, business associate, or friend.

8. *Display inspirational photos* around the computer

screen. Family photos can serve as good reminders of the reasons to avoid sexual content.

9. *Avoid material accessed online* with a cell phone, MP3 player, or PDA. It can be more difficult to block! It you must go online when not using a laptop or desktop computer, make use of your accountability partner to check in before and after.

GOING COLD TURKEY

SOME PEOPLE SIMPLY can't go online at all, at least for a period of time. For example, those in relationships may find that it is too painful for the spouse or partner to see them once again at the computer. For others, online use inevitably leads them to sexual acting out, and they must remain offline indefinitely. Some will not be able to go online at home, but may agree to go to a public place like a coffee shop or library to read e-mail and work. Some cannot even do this.

Being offline or unable to use the computer altogether even for a short period is a very frustrating experience for an adult used to having the freedom to use a computer whenever they wish. When this suggestion has been made, most become quite angry or defensive and describe feeling like a child again. Many try going online again to prove their ability to do so, only to again find themselves in trouble. One porn addict reported:

> *Although I really did feel committed to staying out of my sexual problem areas, it was so easy to pop into a chat room "just to see who was there." I seemed to have endless legitimate reasons to be online, and once there, the porn sites were just a click away. I couldn't seem to stay out of it. Sometimes I would think everything was fine, only to find myself opening unsolicited sexual e-mails and ending up right back where I started. For a while I actually had to*

the house and give it to a friend.
could guarantee to myself that I
ut. Once this was in place I worked
help identify my vulnerable times
nderstand where I need support.
't brought the computer back into
I miss it less and less, especially as
my e-mail when over at a friend's
ids my problem.

TO
CHANGE

READING this book is a good step toward
forward momentum involves rolling up
ting to work. Outlined below are some of
o take toward lasting sexual health.

nning

To remain out of sexual problem areas over time, you must create
a bottom-line definition of the sexual behaviors you are going to
stop. One term for this is *sexual sobriety*. Recovering alcoholics
can clearly define their sobriety as total abstention from the use
of alcohol and other mind-altering chemicals. Their sobriety
date is marked as the date that they gave up drugs and alcohol.
Thus the recovering alcoholic has a clear start date from which
to measure the length of his or her healing process.

A definition of sobriety for a porn abuser or sex addict is also
necessary. Unlike sobriety from the use of substances, however,
sexual sobriety is rarely considered to be complete abstinence
from sex. Some may use complete sexual abstinence for short
periods of time (also see "About Abstinence" in this chapter).
However, they use it as a tool toward healing, not as their final
goal. Sexual sobriety is often defined as a written contract
between the person with the problem and their accountability

partner. These contracts, or "Sexual Boundary Plans," involve clearly stated sexual behaviors from which you are committed to abstain. One man related:

> In my head I knew what I needed to change and how I needed to change it. But somehow I always ended up fooling myself and getting back into trouble. In the moment, I would somehow justify why something was OK for me to do, even though I had previously said that it wasn't OK. It wasn't until I wrote down what I needed to change, and committed to this with another person present, that I found the accountability and clarity to remain sober from my cybersex behaviors.

A Comprehensive Sexual Boundary Commitment

THE UNDERLYING FOUNDATION of any sexual planning must be a set of goals, beliefs, needs, and principles that consistently support the plan itself.

As a part of writing out the detailed sexual sobriety plan, you will first list all the reasons why you want to make changes in your sexual behavior. Then, having stated your personal goals, you will create a sexual boundary plan representing the addictive problem and related areas that need attention.

GOALS

Here are typical goals that underlie a Sexual Boundary Plan. Your actual goals may differ to reflect your circumstances.

Typical Goals (underlying guides to my sexual arousal plan)

- I don't want to have secrets from my family.
- I want to feel like a whole person with integrity.
- I don't want to collect, hide, or pay for pornography.

- I never want to have sex outside of my primary relationship/marriage.
- I want to regain trust with my partner/wife and don't want to put that at risk again.
- Over time, I want to be a man of integrity.

These are the overall guides to your sexual boundary plan. A simple path toward defining porn abuse and sexual sobriety begins by identifying those sexual or romantic activities that cause shame, those that are kept secret, and any behaviors that are illegal or abusive to others.[17] All successful sexual recovery plans have clearly defined, written boundaries.

Some plans start out as simple statements such as "No viewing of sexual images, soft or hardcore" or "No going online for any reason except my work." Another simple one states, "I am sober as long as I do not pay for sex in any form." The important point here is to simply start somewhere and then be accountable to your plan by sharing it with a neutral person who is fully acquainted with your problem.

Here are the typical goals that underlie a sexual boundary plan. Your actual goals may differ to reflect your circumstances.

Detailed Sexual Boundaries Plan

Over time, most people find they need a more elaborate set of guidelines that help guide their healing. Below is a description of such a plan followed an example.

INNER BOUNDARY

The absolute definition of your sobriety—the porn and sexual behaviors you want to stop. Placed within this boundary are the most damaging and troublesome behaviors that need to be stopped immediately. These behaviors (not thoughts or fantasies) are used as a bottom line to define sobriety time; if you do any of these, you have had a slip.

These must absolutely include, but are not limited to: illegal sexual activities; a sexual activity that dismisses the rights of others; compulsive sexual activities that repeatedly threaten your emotional or physical health; and sexual or romantic situations that violate agreements or commitments made to partners or loved ones.

MIDDLE BOUNDARY

Warning signs or situations that can lead you back to pornography abuse and sexual acting out. This set of boundaries lists people, places, and experiences that can trigger you to act out sexually. This area helps to define the situations that "set up" problematic sexual activity. It is not a list of sexual activities themselves but is more a definition of "warning or danger signs."

Examples that belong on this list might be certain hotels you have stayed in where you know you can watch porn; letting soft core pornography (like lingerie catalogs) sit around the house; or e-mailing people with whom you have had a previous flirtatious exchange. This is a list of situations to avoid, a reminder of when to be on guard. Also included on this list are nonsexual issues, which can build up the stress that leads to compulsive behavior. Overwork, lack of sleep, poor self-care, excessive worry over finances or certain family relationships—all are contributing stressors which lead people to act out sexually and belong on this list.

OUTER BOUNDARY

Positive rewards and ways to maintain your sexual boundaries. This final list should offer hope and a vision of improvements and positive things to come. It should list all the activities, hopes, and dreams you have for yourself, whether new or old, now that you are not using porn or sexually acting out. All the time and energy that went into masturbation, finding porn, scanning sites on the Internet, cruising, flirting, or sexual acting

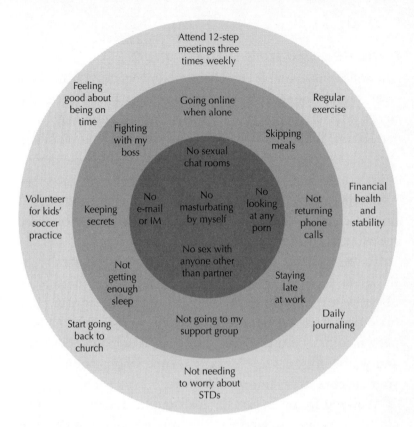

out can now be put to other purposes The items for this list can be immediate and concrete, such as "working on my house, spending more time with my kids" or they may be long-term and/or less tangible such as "beginning to really understand my career goals, studying meditation, and journaling" or "having a better relationship with my spouse."

This list should reflect a healthy combination of work, recovery, and play. If exercising every other day, going to support groups three times a week, and seeing a therapist weekly is going to go on your list, then these need to be equally balanced with spending time with friends, going to the movies, and creative hobbies. Healthy pleasures need to take some of the place of the intensity of sexual acting out.

Sample Sexual Boundary Plan

The following example may help guide you in creating your own Sexual Boundary Plan. All plans vary according to the needs and situation of the individual. Some areas may seem redundant, but it is more helpful to be extremely thorough and detailed in defining a plan rather than general. These definitions should always be reviewed first with at least one other recovering person, therapist, or other safe person and should not be changed later without consulting with one of these individuals.

Partners are not usually the best people to help with this, as these issues are far too personal and sensitive for them to be objective. However, once you have arrived at a clear plan, your mate does have the right to know your boundaries. The best person to help you establish your plan is someone objective and willing to stand up to you; someone who is not afraid of your anger or of hurting your feelings.

Working from the sample goals outlined above, let's now create a sexual boundary plan that might match and enhance these specific concerns and interests. Note that we have included not only sexual things to be avoided, but also some positive things to move toward. Both are important in the development of a Sexual Boundary Plan.

MY SEXUAL BOUNDARY PLAN

USE THIS SPACE to write down your sexual boundary plan. Once it is complete, review this plan with an accountability partner. You will need to approve it together and you will each sign it to show your commitment. The date you sign the plan is your sobriety date. Every day that you stick to your Inner Boundary plan, you are sober.

Once your plan is signed, changes cannot be made to your plan without first discussing it with your accountability partner.

My Goals

Overall guides to my sexual boundary plan

1.   4.
2.   5.
3.   6.

My Inner Boundaries

The absolute definition of sobriety—the porn and sexual behaviors I want to stop

1.   4.
2.   5.
3.   6.

My Middle Boundaries

Warning signs or situations that can lead me back to pornography abuse and sexual acting out

1.   4.
2.   5.
3.   6.

My Outer Boundaries

Positive rewards and ways to maintain my sexual boundaries

1.   4.
2.   5.
3.   6.

My Signature: _____

Accountability Partner's Signature: _____

Date Signed: _____

My Sobriety Date: _____

Remember, it is best if your accountability partner is a sponsor from a 12-step or therapy group, a therapist, or a clergy member.

ABOUT SEXUAL ABSTINENCE

YOU MAY BE so caught up in the compulsions and rituals of your sexual behavior that you really need to take time out from sex altogether in order to clarify what to change and what to work toward. If you have spent the bulk of your adult life in endless patterns of flirtation, sexual obsession, and fantasy, you may need a time-out to learn a sense of your personal strengths beyond simply being sexual to get attention. Not surprisingly, once you stop your problem sexual behaviors, you may find yourself unexpectedly feeling vulnerable, irritable, or anxious, even in familiar situations. These are likely the emotions you previously masked with sexual activity. Much like the newly sober alcoholic who doesn't know how to act at a party without drinking, by becoming sexually abstinent you are forcing yourself to deal with your underlying fears of intimacy, lack of relationship control, and loneliness—all of which are masked by the excessive and addictive use of pornography, mastur-bation, and sex with strangers.

The task of abstinence itself is actually quite simple. Absti-nence simply means abstaining from sex with oneself or anyone else for a committed period of time. It means stopping all sexual activity. This includes looking at any pornography, any type of masturbation, even sex with spouses or partners. Often most helpful in the early stages of the healing process, abstinence is most useful when limited to thirty to ninety days, though it is best to take this time-out in blocks of a month or a even few weeks at a time. Again, this time-out is not a solution for a compulsive sexual problem, but rather a trial period of cleansing and reflection, toward the real goal of integrating healthy sexuality as defined in the sexual boundary plan.

Abstinence commitments should be placed in written form and committed with another person, as in the sexual boundary plan. Accountability is required for any change in sexual behavior, including abstinence.

A FEW FINAL TIPS ON SEX PLANS

1. *Sex plans are flexible;* they are not set in stone. You may spend a month or two with a particular set of boundaries and decide that they need adjustment or changing. This is typical for the recovery process. When making up a plan, don't think *forever,* just think *for now.* Otherwise it can be overwhelming.

   However, changing a sexual boundary plan is not something to be done on your own; making changes involves engaging the help of someone who fully understands your sexual problems and their context. Also, changes to your sexual boundary plan should never be made because some "special" situation presents itself and you decide in the moment that it is time to change your plan. That is not called changing your plan: that is called "acting out," and you would likely have to restart your sobriety time as a result.

2. *If you are looking to justify* or fight to continue a particularly exciting sexual behavior, even though deep down you know that it is not right for you and no longer serves you, you will always be able to find someone willing to allow it and agree that it was "never a big deal anyway." Remember that the idea of creating this plan is not to justify or rationalize your previous behaviors (or some version or them), but rather to bring your sexual acting out to a close.

   So when looking for someone to help with your boundary plan, make sure it is someone who fully understands your history, your concerns, and the future you want to create; someone who is willing to tell you the truth and is not afraid of your response. Also in the beginning it is not a bad idea to be a bit conservative about your sexual choices—you can always loosen up your plan later. When you make a sexual boundary plan, be fully honest with yourself and others about your intentions, remembering your long-term goals and truths.

3. The reason for a concise sexual boundary plan is to hold you accountable to your commitments, particularly in the face of challenging circumstances. One difficulty addicts have is in maintaining a clear focus on their enduring personal beliefs, values, and goals when they are presented with situations that potentially involve intensity and arousal. Unless you clearly follow the defined written boundaries found in your recovery plan, you are vulnerable to deciding "in the moment" what choices are best. Unfortunately, most impulsive decisions do not lead toward long-term goals and beliefs. Maintaining a sexual boundary plan will keep you focused on your healing goals regardless of the situation or a momentary motive.

4. Those in a current marital or romantic relationship who are now creating new sexual boundaries will need to look at how these decisions are going to affect your mutual sex life. For couples, the way the sexual boundary plan evolves will depend in part on the sexual and romantic life you wish to develop together. (Relationships, dating, and sexual healing will be discussed more thoroughly in upcoming chapters.)

೧

SOME OF THE suggestions above will be acceptable to some people and not to others. Some will cringe at the idea of placing written limitations on their sex life. Some will say that it will get in the way of spontaneity or intimacy. This may be true. Some of these steps may even seem contrived or trivial. Keep in mind that that *learning to tolerate your discomfort with change is a major part of growth*. Living in health, without shame, is the goal, and new ideas—even the uncomfortable ones—may serve you better than the practices you have been using. The most important thing you can do to heal may be the one thing that didn't occur to you, so taking on potentially uncomfortable suggestions will likely pay off in the long run.

ABOUT WITHDRAWAL

WHEN QUITTING SUBSTANCES taken regularly for some time, many drug addicts face a variety of withdrawal symptoms, both physical and emotional. Those abusing pornography and sex also have the potential for some uncomfortable withdrawal symptoms when they stop or alter their long-practiced sexual behavior patterns.

This experience can vary in type and intensity from person to person, but some common characteristics of withdrawal are outlined below. If you recognize these in yourself, it is important to talk about them with others—an accountability group, 12-step sponsor, therapist, or friends and family who understand what you are going through. Your discomfort is normal, but if experienced in the extreme, it should be brought to a professional therapist as soon as possible.

Common withdrawal symptoms include:

HONEYMOONING

In the first stages of change, you may lose all craving to look at pornography, compulsively masturbate, or go online for sex: It can feel like you have been cured! You may be excited or intrigued by insight you are gaining, shocked to have finally found a possible solution to your long-term problems, or still be in shock from whatever crisis caused you to examine your behavior in the first place; all can cause a temporary absence of the desire for your former sexual behaviors.

While this break can be a gift and an opportunity to gain knowledge, support, and direction, it can also be confusing, because the desire to act out will certainly return, likely stronger than ever. If this is not anticipated, it is easy to think that something went wrong, when actually the return of these feelings is a very normal part of the process. Healing doesn't mean the feelings of wanting to sexually act out are going to go away. It does mean that they can lessen as you learn how not to act on them.

SWITCHING

It is not unusual for those with histories of sexual acting out to switch their compulsive behavior from the sexual to other forms of problem behavior. One common situation is the man who stops masturbating to porn but begins to eat compulsively and quickly gains weight. Others may return to addictions long ago left behind such as smoking cigarettes or using marijuana.

LONGING AND CRAVING

For most, sexual acting-out behaviors have masked long-held underlying emotions such as depression or grief. Without constant sex as a distraction, these emotions may now manifest themselves as unbearable loneliness, neediness, or unhappiness. You may long for some relationship you fear you will never have, or feel that there is something missing that you cannot find or locate.

These feelings are very normal and to be expected. You are grieving the loss of an adaptive coping mechanism. However, if you find yourself avoiding daily responsibilities such as work or other commitments, taking poor care of yourself, or actually having fantasies or plans of suicide, it is essential to get professional help.

IRRITABILITY

It is typical for withdrawal to evoke a great deal of irritability and anger over what to others are normal, ordinary annoyances. Just as some emotions previously masked by sexual obsessions are depressive, others can be those of anger or frustration. If you can tolerate these feelings without getting fired or kicking the cat, there is much to be learned here. It is common for people who sexually act out to avoid certain types of confrontation and stuff their angry feelings. Learning what provokes your anger and how to manage it is a first step toward better self-care and better relationships. People in withdrawal are not always fun to be around, but it is essential for them to experience, tolerate, and survive these early difficult emotions.

ABOUT SEXUAL ADDICTION

While some pornography addicts are addicted solely to the intensity and arousal provided by images, films, and online sites, you may discover that your sexual problems go much further. It is not unusual, when doing this work, to identify other, perhaps longer-term, problems with addictive sexual behaviors. You may discover through writing and self-examination that you have taken advantage of multiple relationships just to have sex or that you have a compulsive masturbation problem.

A previous history of compulsive masturbation to porn videos and magazines often predates or accompanies computer-porn addiction. Your history could also include having sex with anonymous partners in adult bookstores, seeing prostitutes, having sensual massages, or even the habit of constantly objectifying and sexualizing everyone you see. In the early stages of healing, it is not unusual to recognize and have to face long histories of hidden and secretive sexual problems. As you progress in your recovery, learning to avoid these compulsive sexual behaviors will need to be incorporated into your overall plan.

THE GIFTS OF HEALING

RECOVERING FROM THE effects of pornography abuse and sexual addiction can foster a rediscovery of yourself. Time formerly spent on obsessive online cruising, flirtation, and "the hunt" may now go into family involvement and work. Creativity previously used up in searching for "the hottest" images can now go into hobbies, self-care, and healthier relationships. If you are married or in a committed relationship, healing will bring deeper understanding of both your own and your partner's emotional needs and wants, while encouraging you to take more risks toward vulnerability and intimacy.

Honesty, integrity, and self-knowledge slowly replace hiding and superficiality. The process offers a deepening level of maturity and hope for truly loving relationships previously unknown to those struggling with sexual problems. If you are not in a committed relationship, you can begin to discover true self-esteem by making healthy choices regarding commitment, dating, and romantic partnering, and developing clearer definitions of healthy sexuality personal boundaries. Efforts made toward change now will pay big dividends over time if you are willing to do the work.

Many people don't know where to turn. He next chapter will provide direction and guidance for finding the help you need.

CHAPTER 8

Finding Help

ANYONE WHO HAS spent time in an addiction support group knows that the first steps toward healing involve acknowledging the need for help. Whether you have been an isolated porn abuser or are the spouse of a porn addict, the road to change is best not taken alone.

This chapter provides an overview of places where you can get the help necessary for long-term change; whichever one you choose is a good place to start. You'll also learn how to maintain long-term change, navigate slip-ups, and avoid relapses.

TWELVE-STEP SUPPORT GROUPS

ONE OF THE most useful and utilized tools for healing from substance and behavior addictions is the 12-step–based self-help program. Twelve-step sex addiction meetings offer opportunities for peer support, shame reduction, and guidance, along with an ongoing model for hope and change. Small wonder that groups modeled after the Twelve Steps of Alcoholics Anonymous (AA) help millions recover, one day at a time, from alcoholism and other addictions such as pathological gambling, eating disorders, and sex and porn addiction. Yet walking into your first meeting can be one of your most difficult challenges.

Despite the usefulness of these programs, some object to attending or participating in this type of support group. Whether out of shame, fear of discovery, or the misperception that 12-step groups represent some kind of cult, many would rather "go it alone" than attend a 12-step program. Unfortunately, going it alone is exactly what got most pornography abusers and sex addicts into trouble in the first place. While not all the answers to healing from addiction lie in regular attendance at 12-step meetings, the principles offered by the Twelve Steps, the direction and fellowship of the recovery process, and the support they offer should not be dismissed or ignored as an essential recovery tool. It is strongly suggested that all who are serious about wanting to stop compulsive sexual behavior attend 12-step sexual recovery meetings often (at least as often as they were sexually acting out), begin regular contact with people there who can help, and involve themselves in the group healing process.

For many, just getting to their first meeting is the hardest part, which stems more from anxiety and lack of experience than from anything that actually occurs there. In order to help, some members offered their answers below to some frequently asked questions about 12-step sexual recovery programs and attending meetings. Those answering these questions came from several of the different sexual recovery 12-step programs such as Sex Addicts Anonymous (SAA), Sexual Compulsives Anonymous (SCA), Sexaholics Anonymous (SA), and Sex and Love Addicts Anonymous (SLAA).

Support groups for partners and significant others function like Al-Anon, the group for family and friends of alcoholics. Some of these groups, such as Co-Sex and Love Addicts Anonymous (CO-SLAA), Codependents of Sexual Addiction (COSA), or S-Anon, can be found through the same communities as the support meetings or online (see Resources for more information). However their actual meetings are separate from the 12-step groups for the sex addicts and as such are attended independently. See Resources for complete 12-step program information.

I am concerned about being seen at these meetings and people talking about me because I have been there. How private is a 12-step meeting?

Ironically, it is often the same person who has risked destroying a relationship or even arrest through their sexual behaviors who balks at the idea of walking into a sexual recovery meeting for help. While it is true that the meetings are not bound to the same level of confidentiality as a therapy group might be, all participants of 12-step programs are committed to anonymity as a part of their own recovery process. Many sexual recovery meetings are "closed," meaning available to sex addicts only, which can add an extra layer of safety to attending them. In almost every case the benefits of attending a meeting far outweigh the possible negative consequences. Remember that whoever might see you there doesn't want to be talked about outside the meeting any more than you do.

I don't want to have to talk about myself publicly. Will they make me do this if I go to these meetings?
Other than introducing yourself by your first name only, participation in the meetings is entirely voluntary. No one will make you share anything that you don't wish to.

I have heard that a lot of freaks and sex offenders go to these meetings. My problems haven't really hurt anybody but myself and I don't think I will feel comfortable around a bunch of sex offenders.
A wide range of people attend sexual recovery meetings, from those who are court mandated and there because of illegal behaviors to those involved in problems that are harmful to no one but themselves. Believe it or not, there is something to gain from hearing almost everyone's story at the meetings. At the end of each meeting

you can decide whom you would like to get to know better and whom you want to avoid; whose example you want to follow and whose example doesn't make sense for you.

I have heard that there is a lot of emphasis in these meetings on religion. I don't feel comfortable with all that God stuff and certainly don't want to trade my sexual problems for being involved in a cult. What is the deal with this?
Many people credit their involvement with 12-step programs for having helped to save their lives and relationships. To that extent there can be a bit of fervor about the program by those for whom it has great meaning. But nothing is asked of the newcomer beyond the willingness to simply attend and take whatever works for them personally. The Twelve Steps themselves do use the word *God*. However, this reference is not directed toward any specific religious system, but is rather a reference to spirituality and the idea of reaching out for help to something that is bigger than oneself.

I hear that more people get picked up for sex in those meetings than actually get well. Is it true that sex addicts' meetings are big places to hook up with people looking for sex?
If your goal is to seek sex, you know that you can pretty much find it anywhere. If you go to the 12-step meeting looking for the support of people who have long periods of sexual healing, who can reach out a hand to help you, then that is what you will find. If you go to the 12-step meeting in pick-up mode, you may be able to persuade someone to be sexual with you. In general, the meetings are safe, supportive places. It is always best to get together with new members only in public, staying at the meeting

places or perhaps a coffee shop; it is also best to avoid getting too involved with one member too quickly, as intense relationships are often a hallmark of sexual and romantic addiction.

Q: What is a sponsor and how do I choose one?
A: Sponsors are personal guides to healing and staying sober, usually not friends to begin with and never lovers. A sponsor is usually someone of the same gender as you who has been involved with the 12-step sexual recovery program long enough to have achieved some success. He or she should be active in the recovery meetings, and have worked through the Twelve Steps and written them out. You choose a sponsor by listening to various people at the meetings until you hear someone or several people who seem to meet those descriptors. In addition, they should somewhat match your personal situation so that they can help guide you more individually. For example, if you are married with kids, a sponsor who is also married might be preferable. If you are HIV positive, for example, it might be helpful to have an HIV-positive sponsor. Approach the person before or after a 12-step meeting and ask, "Are you available to be a sponsor and, if so, would you like to have coffee or meet up?" This is the best way to start. If they say no, don't take it personally or give up; just ask someone else.

GETTING INTO THERAPY

GETTING THERAPY IN conjunction with healing from sexual compulsivity can be one of the most helpful steps you can take in early recovery. The therapy setting can provide a safe place to discuss the feelings and initial challenges to ending sexual acting out. Therapists can also serve initially as accountability partners as well as objective guides toward self-awareness. Understanding how you came to engage in these sexual behaviors and what deeper meaning they might have for you is essential to healing. However, finding the right therapist can be half the battle. In the past, incorrect medical diagnoses were often used to categorize sexually impulsive and addictive behavior. There still exists much prejudice and misunderstanding about what constitutes healthy sexuality.

Consequently, arriving at the right therapist to treat pornography abuse or addiction is difficult, but not impossible; fortunately there exist networks of professionals who have been trained to treat sexual addictions and compulsive sexuality.

One common problem encountered by a person seeking help for addictive sexual behavior has been finding himself or herself in treatment with someone more invested in enabling the sexual behaviors than in stopping them. It is not helpful to have a well-meaning supportive counselor offer advice such as, "Maybe you're being too hard on yourself" or "You should just loosen up and allow yourself to become more comfortable with that," or "That's just what guys do," even when the sexual activities described were creating distress and negative consequences for you. Although this may be a good therapeutic tool for those with other kinds of sexual problems, this well-intended advice is exactly the wrong approach for persons whose lives have become increasingly interrupted by intrusive sexual patterns.

Carl relates this story:

Even after I lost a job I really liked because I was using the computer at work for sex, it was hard to get my therapist or any of my friends to take the issue seriously. All of the hours I should have been preparing for the next day or just plain sleeping I was either online masturbating to porn, hanging out in the chat rooms or hooking up for sex. During workdays I was either too tired or too irritable to

*concentrate. Instead I would slack off and try to get away
with doing less or just leave early. Looking back now, I can
see that I needed someone to help me stop those behaviors
and challenge me on my thinking. At the time it was really
easy to agree with what everyone was telling me. I wanted
to believe that what I did was the same as everyone else,
even though deep down I knew it wasn't. It's hard to blame
other people, though, because I'm not sure I was willing to
listen at the time either.*

*The counselor I went to didn't seem to see a problem with
my sexual behavior—he just saw me as a single man with
a healthy sexual appetite. Despite my complaints about the
time, energy and sometimes physical injury my masturbation habits were causing me, he just kept insisting that
I shouldn't be so hard on myself, that I was struggling
with "integrating my sexuality" and that when I was more
self-accepting, I would feel better about my masturbation
habits. Finally after several months of this and only getting
worse, I asked to see someone else.*

∾

IF YOU EXPERIENCE a similar situation, it is important that
you discuss this with your therapist or seek someone trained in
sexual addiction and recovery. Despite the widening evolution
of the field, pornography abuse and sex addiction remain
poorly understood disorders, even by many mental health
professionals. Although nearly twenty-five years have elapsed
since the publication of Dr. Patrick Carnes' groundbreaking
book, *Out of the Shadows: Understanding Sexual Addiction,*
many professionals, including sex therapists, are unfamiliar
with treating any type of addictive sexual behavior. Sex therapists, in particular, are more trained to help people who have

problems enjoying or engaging in sex, rather than those who are addicted to it.

Because there are many different types of helping professionals, choosing the right one can be confusing. These choices include: psychiatrist (M.D.), psychologist (Ph.D.), master's level counselor, licensed social worker (M.S.W.), addiction counselor, licensed marriage and family therapist (M.F.T.) or pastoral counselor. When choosing more important than their specific academic degree is that the counselor you are considering has some training in and knowledge of sex addiction, or at least an understanding of the treatment of addictive disorders.

Keep in mind that the person you choose as your therapist should *never be a friend, neighbor, or family member.* Despite their potential good intentions or even offers for free or low-cost help, it is unethical for psychotherapists or counselors to enter into a professional relationship with someone they know. It is also highly discouraged to barter or trade goods or other services for psychotherapy. It is best to see someone who is well recommended whom you do not know, and to use cash, insurance, or a combination of both to pay for your treatment.

A good place to start looking for a therapist is at the 12-step sexual recovery meetings. By listening to and spending time with other sex addicts in recovery you can get a sense of what is working for them. Many such people may already have counselors or treatment centers where they have successful, supportive therapeutic relationships. Most recovering people, if asked, will be happy to tell you about their therapy experiences and offer helpful recommendations.

Another excellent source of referrals is The Society for the Advancement of Sexual Health's Web site (www.sash.net). It maintains a list of professionals knowledgeable about sex addiction, organized by country and state. Therapists who have expertise in sex addiction are those most likely to be able to help you, but even then you will need to discuss with them their understanding of pornography or online sexual problems.

Many of the nationally known drug and alcohol treatment centers maintain lists of therapists who are trained in sexual disorders and addiction treatment. Addiction treatment facilities can provide names of knowledgeable therapists in your community, as do the gay and lesbian community centers found in most urban areas of the United States and Canada.

Many larger corporations and most unions offer workers access to an employee assistance program (EAP). EAP counselors often have addiction training, though they may not be knowledgeable about sex addiction. If you have health insurance, you need to check your insurance plan to see what diagnoses are covered and which therapists you can use.

Many plans unfortunately do not cover treatment for sexual issues. However, people suffering from pornography abuse and sex addiction often also struggle with anxiety, depression, and work or relationship problems, and you can request referral to a therapist for those issues.

Evaluating a Therapist

The most important part of your evaluation of a perspective therapist is how meeting with him or her makes you feel. Do you feel understood? Do you feel that this person has the knowledge to help you? Do you feel that the therapist is being genuine when meeting with you, or trying to impress you? Is the therapist taking the time to really listen to you, or more interested in hearing him- or herself talk?

QUESTIONS TO ASK A
PROSPECTIVE THERAPIST

To determine whether a therapist is able to handle pornography and sex addiction issues, while also being at ease with you personally, evaluate the therapist's experience by asking questions. *Don't be afraid to ask a prospective therapist questions about training, background, professional orientation, and past work.* The length of time that treatment may take, frequency of treatment, and fees should also all be openly and comfortably discussed. The initial meeting does not, however, commit you to continue therapy with that person. You may wish to "interview" several people before you make up your mind as to which professional might best meet your needs. Like addiction to alcohol, sex addiction is best addressed by addiction treatment, which does differ from traditional therapy.

Consider asking prospective therapists:

- Do you understand pornography abuse and sex addiction?
- Have you ever treated a sex addict?
- What is your experience with sex addiction, with compulsive behaviors in general, with other addictions?
- Do you recommend that your clients attend 12-step meetings?
- Are you familiar with the concepts taught in Alcoholics Anonymous and related programs?
- Are you comfortable and familiar with treating sexual issues?
- How would you help me become accountable to my sexual goals?
- How would you help me if I acted out sexually?
- If applicable: Are you experienced with lesbian, gay, bisexual, or transgender clients?
- If applicable: How will you address or handle my religious beliefs?

Therapeutic Choices

While many therapists prefer to work one-on-one in individual therapy with clients, once a client has been fully evaluated, *the preferred method of treatment for most addictive behaviors is group therapy.* If a therapeutic sex or pornography addiction group is not available, many aspects of the 12-step support group can be used to supplement individual therapy. Seeing an outpatient therapist while attending supportive 12-step sexual recovery meetings works quite effectively for most people. Others are committed to work only within a faith-based or Christian approach that offers accountability and support.

Some people who are experiencing a severe emotional or life crisis related to their sexual acting out, or are unable to stop sexually acting out despite professional help and other support, may require a residential, inpatient, or outpatient intensive treatment program. These more involved and rigorous treatment settings offer a more intensive level of care than simply going to sessions at a therapist's office and attending 12-step or faith-based meetings; they are designed for those who are struggling and in a crisis or who have already unsuccessfully tried a lesser level of care. Even in this case, the first best step is to meet individually with a well-trained professional. He or she can then help guide you through the process.

COUPLES THERAPY

Couples going through a recent discovery that one partner is a pornography abuser or sex addict, or that there has been extensive betrayal by a spouse in the relationship, need a special kind of support. Least helpful is the friend or professional who is reactive or who brings their own preconceived ideas that betrayed spouses "should just leave him" or "kick him out." Many miss the point that partners dealing with betrayal— even on a massive scale—often may not want to give up the relationship over it.

When seeking a couples therapist, it is critical to find someone who can hear your story without having hidden agendas. The porn abuser, so eager to seek forgiveness in the beginning,

NOTE TO THERAPISTS AND HEALING PROFESSIONALS

People who abuse pornography need therapists who understand the addiction. Here are three points to consider when assisting clients:

- The biggest problem among therapists seems to be a lack of information about how behavioral addictions work and what tools are most effective for changing them. Therapists may lack information about types of sexual activities, and sometimes tend to underestimate the tremendous effect of the activity on the user. As a result, therapists may attempt to make the user more accepting of the activity, as in telling compulsive masturbator that "masturbation is normal" without specifically addressing how masturbation works in that person's life, or by telling a patient that they can keep doing what they are doing but need to show more discipline and willpower. Therapists need to ask probing, specific questions about the patient's sexual activity, which will give them a full picture of what the patient is doing and how it is affecting his or her life, with insight into the addictive process.

- Therapists of pornography addicts make another error when they fail to make it a priority to stop illegal or self-destructive behaviors. For example, a young man who is involved in sexual chat and cybersex with underage girls needs help to understand the origins of his behaviors, thereby reducing his sense of shame and self-hatred, but *first* the therapist must insist that this man immediately stop all online sexual behavior.

- A third problem among therapists is the failure to understand fully the degree to which spouses and partners are affected by the porn problem. It is essential to involve the addict's significant other in therapy, whether with the same or a different counselor, and to suggest attendance at support groups if such are available.

For those who are willing and motivated to change their behavior, a knowledgeable therapist or counselor can help them successfully adapt to that change. Initial topics to be discussed in counseling include understanding how the addictive behavior enables the person to cope, acknowledging the costs of using that particular behavior to reach the desired goal, finding alternative means of tolerating difficult circumstances or feelings, and understanding how the person came to use the particular behavior.

When the behavior harms another person, such as the client's spouse or significant other, that person may be brought into counseling as well. The couple may then negotiate ways to get past the pain and difficulties caused by the behavior and develop more productive and positive ways of relating. Therapists must utilize multiple resources to help these clients, including: psychoeducation, written materials, and 12-step or faith-based support groups.

needs the therapist's help to contain their anxiety and fear of abandonment, so that the very partners they betrayed in the first place don't end up having to soothe and reassure them.

The right professional can help the couple negotiate the early stages of recovery, directing the abuser/addict toward the required structure and help, while encouraging the spouse to educate him- or herself about the issues while gaining support for the hurt and anger that they are feeling. The therapist can guide the process of disclosure, helping to reduce the power of long-held sexual secrets.

One recovering person talks about the experience of couples therapy work:

> In the beginning the therapy allowed me access to truths about our relationship that had been covered up for so long. As much as I hated hearing it, I needed to know everything that he had lied about, and the disclosure process was essential. It helped me stop blaming myself so much and allowed me to see the kind of problem Richard had, even before he met me. Later in the therapy, when I wasn't so angry, I began to examine how closed off I had become to him and to myself, how I had slowly accepted living with someone who wasn't emotionally there and what that cost me. I think it really helped us for Richard to be present to hear my end of the story and for both of us to learn what to do differently if we were going to go forward together.

∽

SOMETIMES A COUPLES therapist will see each member of the couple individually for therapy and also see the couple together. More rarely, and usually less successfully, the therapist may see only one member of the couple individually and also see the couple. At some point early on, couples therapy and the therapist's office is a safe place for the addict to disclose his sexual history so that the partner isn't left in the dark regarding what has been going on in the relationship.

It is essential to work with a professional who has a "no secrets" policy. The therapist who holds sexual or related secrets from one partner, while working with both members of the couple, is destined to fail. Though it may be effective to hold onto some information until it is ready to be healthfully disclosed, a good therapist will not promise to keep any secrets over the long term. An effective therapist can help the couple healthfully communicate deep feelings of hurt, loss, and anger. With such sensitive concerns it is best to seek out a therapist who is truly versed in addiction and couples recovery, and who has provided help to couples in the past. Some of the organizations mentioned earlier and in the Resources section can be helpful guides.

FINDING HELP OUTSIDE URBAN AREAS

LIFE IN THE big city offers many opportunities for sexual acting out, but it also offers many places for healing. Large urban areas offer many therapists to choose from and multiple types of 12-step, faith-based, and other daily self-help meetings. People living outside urban areas, however, have fewer supportive resources. Fortunately, this doesn't mean that help is unavailable to those living in less populated areas. Here are some useful suggestions to those living in suburban or more rural environments:

- Several 12-step sexual recovery programs have online meetings and offer long-distance peers and sponsors by phone and/or e-mail communication. Many recovering people participate in regular weekly recovery chats online, while gaining strength and support from around the world. People without Internet access can connect with others by phone. Twelve-step programs also regularly publish newsletters and have other reading materials (available through the mail or online).

- Twelve-step programs also hold annual conventions and conferences in different parts of the United States and around the world. This is a great opportunity to connect with others.

- For sex and porn addicts seeking faith-based help outside urban areas (rather than 12-step–oriented), there are several Web sites that provide information, online support, and telephone counseling. Some of these are listed in the Resources section at the end of this book.

- Some therapists are willing to counsel clients for short periods of time via the telephone or through e-mail exchanges, and many of these professionals can be found online as well.

- A great deal of reading material available devoted to sex addiction is available through online bookstores, libraries, and local bookstores. Also see the Resources section for further reading opportunities.

ABOUT FAITH-BASED RECOVERY FROM PORNOGRAPHY AND CYBERSEX ADDICTION

THERE ARE MANY avenues to recovery from pornography addiction. In this book we have focused mostly on programs based on the Twelve Steps of Alcoholics Anonymous, a tried-and-true method of recovering from addictions and compulsive behaviors. AA is considered a spiritual program, but not a religious one. For people to whom religion is important, there are multiple faith-based resources and strategies for healing. These can be used in conjunction with attendance at 12-step programs, which are compatible with any religious belief system; but understandably, some will wish solely to attend a faith-based program of healing.

We do not recommend approaches that attempt to change a person's behavior by shaming him or her, or by insisting that prayer alone will change the person and eliminate the problem. Fortunately, there are empathetic and non-shaming programs that understand that healing from pornography addiction is not just a matter of willpower but requires direction and accountability, and that porn addicts are not just "morally challenged" people. In the Resources section you with find information on print and Web-based resources for those interested in faith-based healing.

KEYS TO MAINTAINING CHANGE

AS ANY PERSON successfully healing from a compulsive or addictive behavior will tell you, the keys to real behavior change are quite simple. They are:

- Your motivation
- Your willingness to be honest with others and let them help you
- Finding and maintaining accountability

Those who are truly committed to changing their sexual behaviors will go along with sometimes annoying and unfamiliar rituals and situations, experiment with uncomfortable, difficult feelings, and report in to people they barely know—all because they don't want to continue to have their lives driven by addiction. If you have had some external consequence such as an arrest, or a relationship, health, or other personal crisis that has motivated you to commit to no longer defining your life by pornography and sex, then you are among those most likely to stay with the process and see long-term change occur.

If you are running to get help simply to calm an upset partner, accommodate a court order or a boss, or try superficially to feel better about yourself—while continuing to sexually act out in some hidden way—you will discover that it becomes harder and harder to live a double life while gaining self-knowledge and awareness. At some point you will either have to commit fully to the actions suggested toward changing your sexual behavior, or end up returning to the very patterns of sexual insanity you sought to change in the first place.

Making Sense of Slips and Relapse

ROBERT TELLS THE story of how thinking he had solved his sexual problems actually landed him right back where he started:

During the first few months of my healing process, I was involved in therapy, attended multiple weekly 12-step meetings, and regularly worked at learning about and managing my problem. I began to pray and meditate, and open up to healing. I slowly began to regard my past sexual behavior as a symptom of a difficult time in my life that was now ending.

When I passed the nine-month mark of having stopped, I gradually became less serious about some earlier commitments, such as keeping my Internet filters current or not staying at work late alone. I started going to fewer support group meetings and skipping therapy. Somehow, I never had found the time to get rid of that one e-mail address where I used to get porn, though I always said I'd get to it. One Saturday when I was feeling overwhelmed from the work week I thought, "I should really just relax today and take some time for me. I deserve it." So I slept in instead of going to my regular Sunday 12-step meeting. That morning it occurred to me I should just get online to see how well I was really handling the problem.

Within minutes I had hooked my Webcam back up (the one my therapist had told me to throw out weeks ago) and "found myself" engaged in mutual masturbation online with a total stranger. Afterwards, I was shocked at how easily and quickly I seemed to return to my former behaviors. I realized then that unless I consistently and thoroughly followed the plans that had been suggested to me—I wasn't going to get well and stay well.

❧

ROBERT'S STORY DEMONSTRATES that having some success in working on these problems can lead you to slip up if you convince yourself that you have fixed the problem or are cured. Robert didn't overtly start out looking for sex, though by reviewing the situation and writing about it, he can now recall feeling mildly excited about being home alone and feeling entitled to it. He wrote, "I deserve to be able to have this time to myself to go online. I have been working so hard. It's a good reward." Robert's story helps outline some important signs of impending relapse, a return to former problem behaviors.

Key Warning Signs of Relapse

- Overconfidence: "This has gone really well for a few months, maybe I have the problem licked."
- Isolation: Spending several days without contact with other recovering people and without going to support groups or meetings
- Blaming others: "If my boyfriend hadn't gotten a job that took up so much of his time, I wouldn't be so lonely and tempted by other guys."
- Making excuses and setting up slippery situations: "I could leave work with everyone else like I always do, but I think I'm fine now so I will just stay late alone to get this project done."

- Minimizing a return to problematic situations: "It's not like I'm talking to other women anymore, I'm just looking at a few images. Besides, every guy looks now and then."
- Skipping or devaluing feedback from others: "That support group just wants to control me. They are just a bunch of sexually repressed losers. It's too expensive and I'm doing fine on my own."
- Feeling victimized by not having complete sexual freedom: "Every other guy gets to buy magazines, masturbate to movies, and get as much as he wants. I don't see why I should deprive myself, what's the point in that?"
- Ignoring previously agreed-upon guidelines
- Feeling entitled to return to some of the formerly problematic behaviors: "Look how hard I have been working at the office and in my recovery, what difference does it make if look at a few videos here and there, it's not like I have a decent relationship. I deserve something good for me."

∾

YOU MAY RECOGNIZE yourself and your thinking in the warning signs examples. It is actually a part of the process for the problem to "fight back" once in a while as healing occurs. And though not a cause for celebration or to be used as an excuse, slips may occur for some. *A slip* is defined as a brief, mostly unintended return to a former sexual acting out behavior. Sometimes an unexpected stressor, a poorly managed or maintained recovery plan, or other such situation will lead to a sexual slip. However, a slip is not a relapse.

A slip can be managed and contained by immediate, honest disclosure of the event, followed by a revised plan to shore up the desire to avoid acting out. If you are in a relationship, a slip is something you tell your spouse about so that you don't create any new secrets—no matter what the cost. If you are single, slips must be disclosed promptly to sponsors, therapists, and key support people in your life.

Relapse occurs when you are unwilling to be honest about a slip to yourself and others and you begin to hide and justify your behaviors. This sets the stage for them to recur over and over again. *Hidden or ongoing slips, lies, isolation, and a return to a secret hidden sexual life define relapse.*

In the next chapter, learn how to maintain a long-term commitment to healing by taking care of yourself and enjoying life.

CHAPTER 9

Next Steps: Moving Beyond the Problem

THERE IS MORE to healing than simply stopping a problem behavior. The word *recovery* is used in addiction treatment because it implies the healing of your sense of self, life, and creativity. Although the "do's" of the recovery process reviewed in the last chapter are the tools that bring about and maintain change, more must be done to effect your happiness and peace of mind. True long-term healing occurs through a commitment to the practice of self-care and learning to finding the healthy pleasures that make life worthwhile.

This last chapter is devoted to healing and moving on for both singles and couples.

THE IMPORTANCE OF SELF-NURTURING

PEOPLE WITH PROBLEMS often have difficulty taking time out just for themselves or even recognizing that they should. Porn addicts tend to be intensity-focused. Unable to be soothed by long-term meaningful life rewards (such as watching the garden grow or the intimacy of a close partnership develop), active porn abusers leach intensity from external events and experiences for distraction. This is the essence of their pathology.

The feelings of emptiness and inner discomfort that the porn abuser and sex addict previously used sex as a fix, must now be relieved through self-care and self-nurturing. Long-term healing must include learning how to "do nothing" for a day and find hobbies and interests that bring pleasure, fun, and healthy distraction. This part of the process can be so foreign to those healing from pornography problems that it ends up being the hardest.

Similarly, partners of porn and sex addicts often have trouble knowing exactly what makes them happy, as they have often been more focused on meeting the needs of others than fulfilling themselves. Partners of those with problem behaviors are often centered on making sure that everyone around them has their wants and needs met, yet they too often place their own needs last. In the early recovery/healing phase, partners may find themselves similarly focused on what their porn-abusing partner needs to do to get better, rather than on how they can nurture themselves.

In the pages that follow, we will explore ways for those in recovery to nurture themselves, for couples to nurture each other, and we will provide resources for partners.

NURTURING TASKS FOR YOURSELF

Attending to Nonsexual Friendships

Porn abusers and sex addicts who are active in their addiction often have little going on in their personal lives beyond the addictive behaviors themselves. Absorption in their sexual fantasy life prevents them from being aware of any loneliness or isolation they might otherwise feel. Even if they are active socially and appear to be close to others, they feel separated by their sexual secrets and the all-consuming nature of their sexual behaviors. Their partners often find themselves alone, without the support of home and spourse. Those who know about the problem sexual activities often feel too embarrassed to talk about it with friends and other supportive people, and instead remain isolated and unhappy.

Isolation is a hallmark of emotional disease. Every healing

person needs others outside of partners or family with whom they can discuss their painful challenges and losses. This is why participation in therapy, 12-step recovery programs, and other support groups is encouraged. Even though it may be embarrassing at first to discuss such concerns, the support and acceptance that comes with reaching out to a safe person can far outweigh any adverse consequences.

Meditating

Long encouraged by religious groups and 12-step programs, the practice of regular meditation can create more peace and calm within. If the goal is to move away from intensity and arousal as a source of distraction, working to create calm and peace within is the right way to go. Taking classes or finding a good book about meditation is the easiest way to start. Suggested books include *Mindfulness in Plain English*, by the Venerable Henepola Gunaratana (Wisdom Publications); *Wherever You Go There, You Are*, by Jon Kabat-Zinn (Hyperion Publications); and *Answers from the Heart: Meditations for Sexual Addicts*, by Hazelden Meditations (Hazelden Publications).

Exercising

Those who intensely pursue instant gratification through sex usually neglect their physical health and utilize few healthy methods to reduce the stress we all experience. This is why addiction treatment programs typically include physical fitness regimens as an important element of their work. Achieving life balance means paying attention to your emotional, spiritual, and physical health. Aside from all the benefits of physical self-care and weight loss, exercise induces many of the same neurochemical changes in the brain that are produced by arousal- and intensity-based addictions such as sexual acting out—only in a much healthier fashion. Even the simplest exercise routine (like daily walking), used consistently and in a committed fashion, will add significantly to feelings of serenity, peace, and self-care.

Remaining Balanced

The pressures of modern life make it easy for anyone's life to get out of balance, especially those who have relied on sexual behaviors to distract themselves. Over time all the attention goes to the pornography use and not enough to friends, romantic partners, family, children, or the demands of work. Life can become about frantically putting out fires and playing catch-up to commitments that have been ignored at work and at home. Much of the time, life is lived "in overwhelm."

When overwhelmed, the addict's handiest solution in the past was always more pornography, more intensity. The healthy solution is to set appropriate priorities and boundaries for work commitments, self-care, and personal relationships. Establish a plan for the maximum number of hours you will work each week, and prioritize commitments to family, friends, and personal time. This will go a long way toward helping you attain and maintain balance and a sense of control in your life.

Spending Time in Nature

Feelings of isolation and aloneness are often pervasive for those who abuse sex and pornography. Some have felt alone their whole lives. A powerful way of realizing that you are not alone, but rather a part of a vast universe, is to spend some time in nature. Outdoors in nature, the interconnectedness of life is realized—a visit to Mount St. Helens in the northwest United States makes clear the devastation that a volcanic eruption can have upon hundreds of square miles for decades to come, and also the regeneration that is possible. A trip to the Grand Canyon in Arizona shows how over eons water can carve a huge rift in solid rock. A walk in the woods illustrates how birds depend on trees to build their nests, on worms to feed their offspring, on their partner to incubate their eggs. Interdependence, not isolation, is the rule of nature—a good one for recovering people to remember.

Owning a Pet

Medical studies have shown that older people who have pets are happier and healthier than people who don't share their lives with animals. When asked to give an example of unconditional love, most people immediately think of the love of a dog for its owner. Pets can immeasurably enhance the life of their owners. Having a dog or cat to greet you at the door when coming home from work, keep you company when reading or watching TV, or entice you out of the house for a walk can help keep "alone" from becoming "lonely," especially for those who live by themselves. Moreover, caring for the physical and emotional needs of another living being, whether human or animal, can give a different focus to life besides just worrying about oneself.

Hobbies, Sports, Games, and "Having Fun"

The healing process can make it too easy to become so focused on 12-step meetings, therapy sessions, spending quality time with the kids, work, and other previously neglected goal-oriented activities that recreation is often avoided. When life becomes busy and complex, taking time out for travel, hobbies, sports, and other "nonproductive" activities may seem silly. However, recharging your battery provides the self-nurturing that makes you ready again to go out and succeed at work, relationships, and other aspects of life. The key to a productive and psychologically healthy lifestyle is to incorporating play and recreation to help keep your life in balance.

Creating "Home" at Home

When sexual images and arousal are your primary life priority, there is little room to focus on creating a home life that is warm and inviting. While using sexual distraction to ignore their emotional or "inner" selves, porn abusers readily ignore their "outsides" as well. Take the time to put in a garden, paint a guest room, buy flowers weekly, or arrange the furniture. The simple acts of improving your home and taking daily or weekly steps to maintain it reflect an important commitment to taking care of yourself. It provides a reminder of the ongoing positive change that ending an addiction can bring.

FROM SINGLE TO COUPLE: ABOUT DATING

RECOVERY FROM PORNOGRAPHY abuse and sex addiction does not mean avoiding dating, romance, or healthy sexual expression. Once you have gotten through the first six to nine months of active work on your sexual issues, it may be time for singles to begin planning for healthy dating and healthy romance. The safest way to begin this process is by reaching out to those who know you and help hold you accountable, and discussing your feelings and intent toward dating with them. They can help you develop a carefully thought out written dating plan that, like your sexual boundary plan, will provide specific, established guidelines toward how and where best to meet people and how long to date before having sex.

This plan should encourage a path toward emotional intimacy, rather than a return to high intensity, sexually charged behavior. Moving toward healthy sexuality as a single person can be confusing and imperfect, but hopefully by this stage you have found those supportive people who are available to act as your guides and mentors so you don't have to do it alone.

Healthy Dating on the Internet

It is an unavoidable fact that meeting and dating in the twenty-first century is more often than not facilitated by the Internet. This presents some additional problems for those who have had a problematic relationship with the Internet. Here are some tips to help you navigate online dating.

INTENTIONS

Though many sites are not specifically oriented toward sex, overt sexual content can be found anywhere if you are looking for it. If you have found yourself using dating sites to find masturbatory images or to hook up for anonymous sex, it is best to avoid them or use an accountability partner when accessing them. For those who are ready and able to start looking for a healthy partnership, the Internet provides many avenues to do so and we encourage it.

Some dating sites (for example, Match.com and YahooPersonals.com) state they are specifically geared to single people, whereas others openly offer options for NSHM ("not so happily married") people as well. Some dating sites carefully peruse potential clients' personal statements, refusing membership to those who are openly soliciting sex partners, whereas others offer that as an option on their list of goals for the member. Some sites send information about potential partners to members via e-mail; others require members to initiate visits to their Web sites.

SAFETY

Although most people who sign up on dating sites are legitimate, a few are not. It is all too easy, and in fact extremely common, for people to alter key features about themselves, and to disguise their real intentions in soliciting partners. When visiting dating sites, read their anonymity statement, and use

INTERNET DATING SITES

Match.com

GreatExpectations.com

YahooPersonals.com

FriendFinder.com

PerfectMatch.com

Matchmaker.com

AmericanSingles.com

Lavalife.com

eHarmony.com

PerfectSingles.com

Idsingles.com (Christian singles)

Equallyyoked.com (Christian site)

Xianz.com (Christian)

Jdate.com (Jewish singles)

PlanetOut.com
(gay, lesbian, bisexual, and transgender)

Gay.com (gay, lesbian, bisexual, and transgender)

Rightstuffdating.com
(graduates of selected universities)

caution.

It is prudent, therefore, not to disclose addresses, telephone numbers, financial status, or work circumstances. The safest dating sites are those that forward e-mail using a different e-mail address. When using a screen name to enroll in a dedicated dating site, the person being contacted doesn't know your real name or even your actual e-mail address. There are also dating sites that do not list e-mail addresses within profiles, but if someone wants to be in contact, the dating service supplies the actual e-mail address. A dating service that includes one's own e-mail address onscreen is the least safe. When providing a self-description in online profiles, focus on interests and personality characteristics. Do not reveal your place of employment, income, and other personal life details.

After some e-mail exchange, you may feel comfortable enough to give out your telephone number and have a phone conversation. It's a good idea to get the other person's phone number as well, and call him or her. People who are married or lying about other important matters are less likely to give out their phone number.

If choosing to meet in person, public places are best. Telling another friend of your specific arrangement is a good idea. If traveling a long distance to meet someone, it is ideal to have return arrangements in place, meet in a public place, and again advise a friend or family member of the exact plans and schedule.

If meeting someone in a general interest chat room or a dating site (as opposed to a sexually-oriented location), there is reason to be concerned if the person asks intrusive or peculiar questions, seeks sexual information, or wants a phone number without disclosing his or hers.

Also be forewarned about people who are reluctant to divulge details of their life, while probing you for yours, or give you conflicting information about crucial aspects of their life, such as marital status, career, family circumstances, or financial status.

Sooner or later, people getting to know each other online exchange photos. In helping a subscriber decide whether or not to post a photograph with her online profile, Match. com reports that those who do post a picture of themselves do get eight times as many inquiries as those who don't have photos online. Obviously, posting your photograph makes you less anonymous, so some people choose to wait until they are exchanging e-mails.

THE MASK OF ONLINE COMMUNICATION

COMMUNICATING BY E-MAIL is like exchanging regular letters ("snail mail"), only they are transmitted much faster via the Internet than by trucks, airplanes, and the friendly mail carrier. E-mail can be accessed at one's convenience, allowing all the time needed to compose a well-thought-out and well-written reply. E-mail provides the opportunity to present one's best side, taking as long as needed to make changes and adjustments along the way. Unfortunately, e-mail provides the fewest clues about the person, as visual and auditory cues are absent.

One alternative to e-mail is the chat room, which allows for real-time conversation among a group of people, using the medium of typing rather than speech. A variant of the chat room is the private room, where people can converse by typing instant messages to each other. Written exchanges occur much faster in chat rooms or private rooms than they do with e-mail, so there may be more revealed about the person's personality. These days, many people send instant text messages to the recipient's cell phone, so that e-communication is no longer limited to access via the desktop or laptop computer.

Of course, telephone conversations give even more information—allowing a vocal impression well as clues about the other person's ability to listen and empathize. Nothing, however, beats a face-to-face meeting. Many have had the experience of meeting someone for the first time and of knowing within a few minutes that the person was someone they do—or don't—want to see again. Often this is a response to the many visual, emotional, and intuitive cues people unconsciously receive. Despite having exchanged several e-mails or having spent enjoyable time on the phone with someone, there may be a strong negative reaction on an initial face-to-face meeting.

It is important to define the goal of meeting someone online. If, for example, it is to acquire a support system to help work through a life crisis or that of a family member (such as an illness), then online friendships may be the perfect answer. But if the goal is a dating relationship with the possibility of intimacy, then the Internet becomes most useful as an initial screening tool. If your goal is a romantic relationship, avoid a long-term online-only friendship. Once it is established that this is someone safe and interesting enough to get to know better, arrange an offline meeting—in a public place.[18]

TO THE COUPLE: NURTURING TASKS FOR COUPLES

WHILE THE BEGINNING of this chapter offered suggestions for how individuals can heal and nurture themselves as individuals, couples too can learn to nurture each other and their relationship better. These steps are as important a part of creating change for individuals and couples as are the more "serious" parts of the process.

Making Dates for Time Together

In our busy lives it can be easy to let time slip away without really making time for our partnerships. The expected distractions of work, family, kids, recovery, work, and friends can easily take precedence for couples over spending time together alone. Yet studies have proven the need for couples to make the time to be together. This is especially true for couples healing from sexual problems that carry the burden of past pain and betrayal. Although making advance preparations seems unromantic, it is essential that couples *plan* times to spend together. The goal is to make actual dates—unbreakable except in an emergency—for the couple to spend time together in play and relaxation, with or without sex. Whether a trip to the beach or an evening on the town, couples need time apart from stress and distraction for growth and healing.

Listening/empathy

One tool that effectively helps couples become closer is to learning more effective ways to listen to one another and make time for sharing. One way is to set aside several specific times each week for listening to each other. This fifteen-minute exercise is best carried out when the distractions of the day have ended and there are a few quiet moments. The couple sits facing each other. Each person has five minutes of uninterrupted time to say whatever he or she wants to the other person. This can be about their day, feelings, work, and family . . . anything they want to say. Then the other partner takes a turn, spending five minutes speaking without interruption. The last five minutes is designed as a mutual time for both to discuss what they have heard and how they feel about it. Carried out two to three times weekly, this simple exercise goes a long way toward helping couples establish intimacy and closeness.

Sharing Activities

Couples in recovery need to find time to do activities that stimulate and interest one another. Hiking, gardening, playing sports, going to museums, or antique stores are all examples of potentially relationship-growing activities. Experiences that take the couple and/or family out of their daily routine, or simply out of the house for fun, create a bonding and shared intimacy that no therapy session can offer.

Nonsexual Touching and Holding

Many people who have issues with sexuality and porn either

grew up in homes where they had very little touch and experienced little physical intimacy, or else had childhoods where their exposure to intimacy was inappropriate and overwhelming. Children brought up by parents who are physically affectionate also greatly benefit from the healthy closeness and reassurance that this brings. Healthy couples need to work on building physical closeness not necessarily focused on sex. Hand-holding, hugs, cuddling, bathing together, massages, shoulder rubs, and kisses all offer warmth and validation that cannot be bought with words alone.

Introducing Romance

As the couple begins to move toward forgiveness and healing, romantic interactions work to develop intimacy; this does not necessarily mean sex, but rather the actions people take toward one another at the beginning of a new relationship to help each partner feel loved and appreciated. Notes, cards, flowers, unexpected compliments, and surprise gifts and plans all work toward the reestablishment of romance. These activities are better carried out in the later stages rather than early in recovery. They should not to be used by the addict as an attempt to gain quick forgiveness from the partner. Rather, in a partnership where both people have been working toward establishing trust, romantic interactions help bring closeness and warmth back into the relationship.

REBUILDING TRUST

MOST PORN ABUSERS and sex addicts have lied, covered up, manipulated, and hidden their secret lives from those close to them. No wonder loved ones feel betrayed and violated, finding trust difficult—if not impossible. Even when the porn addict adheres to a strict recovery program, studies have shown that it often takes a year or two before their partner ceases to have doubts about their activities. Unfor-

RIGOROUS HONESTY

The best antidote for a past life of secrecy and dishonesty is a present life of rigorous honesty in all areas, small and large. It takes many days, weeks, and months of consistency to overcome the distrust that has been created through their past behavior. Simple things are very meaningful when trying to reestablish trust. For example, if you are going to be late, even a little, phone your partner to explain. If you have agreed to pick up some milk on the way home but forget, it is better to admit having forgotten than to make up some excuse. If there is a need to use the computer at home, it is better to have it in a high-traffic area of the home than to sit at the computer behind a closed door, expecting your partner to "just trust you" or believe that nothing inappropriate is going on.

Nancy, 40 years old, talked about how she gradually came to trust her husband, Nick again:

It's been a gradual process. He's been very trustworthy. He made sure to be home when he was supposed to and made himself available by cell phone, even if I called him several times a day. He would always phone me or leave a note if he had a change of plans. He would sit listening without argument, sometimes for long periods, when I would need to express my anger and disappointment, even though I knew he wanted to defend himself. For a long time he kept on that straight and narrow, even if he had to go out of his way. It took about a year until he didn't need to do that anymore. If he was going to be late, he didn't have to rush to a phone to let me know why; I was no longer sitting at home tapping my fingers and wondering where he was if he was five minutes late. As I got better, I didn't need all those reassurances anymore.

It is essential for the healing of the partners of porn abusers and sex addicts to see the addict/abuser fully engaged in active healing—through regular attendance at self-help meetings, therapy, spiritual work, and by their consistent adherence to the activities that make it safe to have a computer at home (such as leaving it in a public place in the home, installing blocking software, putting time limits on its use, and so on). Ongoing involvement in such activities helps convince the partner that there is real sincerity and commitment to moving past previous sexual problems and changing his or her life.

tunately, some partners never regain confidence in their own judgment about the addict. Clearly, the healing process for a relationship involves many steps toward rebuilding trust and gaining healthy intimacy.

The following are steps that couples can take to help repair a damaged relationship. There are several steps that can facilitate rebuilding trust.

Steps you can take as the former porn abuser or sex addict

- Exhibit daily rigorous honesty with everyone in both small and large issues.
- Work toward greater understanding of the pain you have caused partners and loved ones.
- Allow your partner time to rebuild trust, by letting him or her feel anger and mistrust without expecting an immediate "all is forgiven."

- Avoid apologies and making excuses for past behavior. Simply acknowledging what you have done and not repeating it will offer more than a thousand "I'm sorrys."
- Spend time with your partner doing things that he or she enjoys. This might include going to a movie the partner particularly wants to see, to an art show, or to a baseball game. The willingness to do this demonstrates that what matters to your partner also matters to you.
- Establish and maintain a stable and consistent plan for your own self-care.
- Remain committed to maintaining your clear plan for recovery.

Steps you can take as the partner of a porn abuse or sex addict:

- Educate yourself about addiction—read, take classes, go to support groups
- Commit to your own personal healing and self-care.
- Work toward being less judgmental and critical by showing a greater willingness to acknowledge your part in your challenges as a couple.
- Be willing, *over time*, to grow beyond anger and betrayal and find a path toward trust.

HEALTHY SEXUALITY

SURPRISINGLY, MANY PEOPLE who have had a lot of sexual experience often don't know what constitutes healthy sexuality. This is particularly true of porn addicts and sex addicts. Until the book *Sexual Behavior in the Human Male* (the Kinsey report) was published in 1948, sex was surrounded by great secrecy, and no one really knew what others did behind closed doors. Today we have the opposite situation—an abundance of books claim to teach us how to live sexually fulfilling lives. Television, films, and the Internet provide people with thousands of images (both still and moving) of various forms of sex. Yet people are as confused as ever. Therapy clients often say, "We are trying to find out what a 'normal' sexual relationship is all about."

Porn and sex addicts often misconstrue intensity for intimacy. They have been so focused on immediate arousal and excitement for so long that many lack the understanding that healthy sexuality in a long-term relationship has more to do with relating emotionally and mutual appreciation and less to do with "being horny" or with "hot body parts." Exercises that introduce nonorgasmic and nongenitally focused physical closeness as a vehicle toward sexual intimacy can be found in most books on adult sexual health. Some couples who seek to restore the previous "intimacy" in their relationships will turn to sexual intensity or romantic "honeymoon" experiences as a quick means to recreate some closeness in their relationship following the disclosure of a sex addict's problem.

At the beginning of the recovery process it is not unusual for couples who have had relatively distant, dispassionate sexual relationships to temporarily get into a lot of intense sex with each other. Although sexual intensity may feel good for the moment, providing each partner with some measure of reassurance, sex used to sustain and comfort while avoiding deeper more troubling issues in the relationship is a form of mutual denial that is bound to fail. It is healthier, though less comfortable, to engage in a "cooling off period," agreeing not to cycle into any sexual or romantic intensity, while also avoiding any longer-term decision making—such as whether or not to break up or permanently change residences—until there is more clarity about where things are headed.

Therapists often recommend that a couple take some time—typically thirty to sixty days—during which they abstain from any form of sex. This abstinence period is used to grieve the past, to learn more about addiction and addictive patterns in relationships, to express strong emotions such as anger and guilt and begin healing from them, and to learn how to express affection for each other in nonsexual ways. Porn addicts also use this period to learn that they can survive without sex (see more in Chapter Seven)—something that most porn and sex addicts find hard to believe. During this time the couple attends support groups and individual and couple therapy. They work towards being able to make informed decisions about their relationship.

Later steps involve the couple to begin to formulate what is healthy sex *for them*. We believe that a healthy sexual relationship for recovering people is not exploitive of others, is life enhancing rather than destructive, is enjoyable by both partners, takes place within the context of a caring relationship, and has a spiritual component. The first step to a healthy sexual relationship is to discuss your feelings and desires openly with your partner. Those who have had negative sexual experiences in the past—such as being sexual abused or molested—may benefit from counseling to get beyond the emotional consequences of the experiences. Healing and mutually intimate sexuality is a learned experience that comes from open communication, trust, and shared values.

RECOVERY FOR THE CYBERSEX ADDICT'S PARTNER

PARTNERS, AND THE relationship as a whole, benefit when the partner makes it a priority to work on him- or herself. Although many partners rightly feel that they didn't create the problem and indeed in many ways have been victimized, a great deal of growth can still be achieved by seeking help. Counseling and self-help groups can result in improved self-esteem and less reactivity on the partners' part and are likely to help them become more willing to risk vulnerability with their partner again. This work assists partners in trusting their perceptions and judgment, therefore empowering them. Once they rely on their gut feelings to inform them that something is wrong, they are more likely to risk trusting again.

Nick, Nancy's husband, had affairs both online and offline. Nancy was devastated when she first learned about the repeated betrayals. She felt completely blindsided, having had no inkling whatsoever that the time missing from his schedule had been spent having sex with other women on the computer and in real life. Now, after two years of counseling and 12-step work, Nancy is willing to trust Nick again. The reason is not only that he has acknowledged the problem and has gotten help, but also because she trusts herself more. She says:

> If Nick had another affair, I would leave him. I know that today I would know long before it happened. It wouldn't be like it was before, because I could spot the signs right away, even without any detective work. I'm a different person now, more independent, more sure of myself. Before, I was certain that the kids and I would starve out there. That's what Nick kept telling me, too. Now I have enough faith in my Higher Power that He would get me through.

Empathy and Patience

The process of healing requires both partners to develop greater empathy for the other. Empathy is the ability to feel and relate deeply to what someone else is going through, even if you have not had the very same experience. Going to couples counseling and attending support group meetings with other individuals and couples can help facilitate this process (for suggested groups refer to the Resources section). It can be easier to empathize when hearing the pain of someone else's partner than your own, especially when your partner's upset may have involved behavior that pushed your buttons and invited your anger. Listening to other couples talk about their problems and their efforts to resolve them can help people better understand their own partner.

Pornography abusers often experience an understandable sense of loss and anger at giving up what often felt like a reliable coping tool (getting lost in the porn). They also feel a great deal of shame about their behaviors and cover-up attempts. Sometimes, their own sensitivity and self-judgment may be so overwhelming that they cannot relate to the hurt and sense of betrayal their partners feel. Listening carefully to your partner, reversing roles and role-playing in therapy, and hearing others' stories in support groups can all facilitate the development of empathy. When partners feel that their pain is understood, they are more likely to believe that the cybersex abuser will not hurt them again. Both must be patient; trust and healing come slowly.

Partners of porn and sex addicts are often focused on their own hurt, betrayal, and injury to their self-esteem, for which they blame the porn user. Understandably, they fail to see that giving up the porn is a real loss that their addicted spouse will require working through. They are appropriately angry, but often judgmental as well, seeing the one who sexually acted out as the only one with a problem, while seeing themselves as innocent victims. This adds to the porn abuser's feelings of shame and low self-esteem. Counseling, listening exercises, role-playing in therapy sessions, and listening to others tell their stories can all help build empathy in the partner and melt away judgmental thinking.

Jessica, a 50-year-old critical care nurse, had a very demanding career, which became more demanding when she was promoted to head nurse of the cardiac care unit. Paul, her husband of twenty-five years, had recently retired and became very interested in surfing the Internet on his new computer. Eleven years earlier, Paul had begun a recovery program for sex addiction after admitting to multiple affairs. His problem behaviors had ceased so many years ago, that when Paul began staying up late at the computer, it never occurred to Jessica that he was involved in anything sexual. She noticed that he seemed to lose interest in sex with her, but she was willing to accept this as a consequence of her new work schedule and of a long-term marriage. Eventually he admitted to her that he had begun engaging in cybersex. He was viewing pornography and masturbating, as well as exchanging sexually oriented e-mails with other women online.

Paul resumed active involvement in a 12-step program for sex addiction. He set up guidelines for himself for computer use, such as not using it late at night, and installed blocking software and signed up with a family-oriented Internet service provider (ISP). Jessica was initially furious, but soon realized that some marital issues had predisposed Paul to his relapse. Because she had become preoccupied with her work and left him alone for long periods with unstructured time on his hands, he felt unneeded and unappreciated.

By attending counseling together and making a commitment to daily time sitting and talking, going out on weekly "dates," spending more time together on weekends, and maintaining their own personal recovery steps, Jessica and Paul were able over time to evolve into a new level of intimacy that had never before been a part of their relationship.

Learning to Trust Again

An important gift of healing is the return of trust in yourself. This involves the ongoing monitoring of your instinctive as well as intellectual responses to the sexual stimulation that you are bound to run into in the world and then make the appropriate response. People whose primary focus is arousal and emotional distraction are not free to assess and respond to the world in a healthy way. Their inner life has already been hijacked by the preoccupation and obsession that is characteristic of all addictions.

This is why addicts are often unaware of the damage they have caused and the hurt they have inflicted on others. We call this "denial." Unexpected, bad things just "seem to happen" to them, and they feel buffeted by events rather than being in charge of their own lives. Their "early-warning system" seems to be permanently turned off.

Partners also do not trust themselves. Often they have been so heavily invested in their relationship—sometimes driven by fears of being left behind—that when given a choice between believing their own instincts and conclusions versus a lie told to them by a porn-abusing partner, they all too often will surrender to a deception over their own intuition. They, too, are in denial about what is happening around them.

This is why partners are often the last to know about affairs or other compulsive sexual behavior, even if the activities have been evident to family, neighbors, and friends. Partners are often completely unprepared when they learn about some hidden activity, even though there may have been many clues available. Not surprisingly, they find it difficult to trust others; if they cannot trust themselves, how could they possibly trust others?

An important aspect of healing from sexual betrayal and abuse is to learn to pay attention to the signals coming in from the outside world, and most importantly, to one's own gut reactions. When you trust yourself, using our own reactions as a guide to our responses, the world no longer seems so unpredictable. Events don't "just happen." We feel in greater control and have less of a need to control others. Learning to trust yourself is a prerequisite for negotiating the world with confidence and faith.

LAST WORDS

WHILE FOR SOME pornography has provided a path to sex education, play, and healthy stimulation, there are many who find its distractions destructive to their beliefs, self-esteem, and relationships. Most who find pornography unpalatable or problematic can simply choose to avoid it as best as possible, keeping it out of their personal lives and relationships. However, there are those who seem to have lost the ability to choose when or even if they wish to use pornography. For these people and those close to them, engaging with sexual images, videos, stories, Internet chat, and virtual sex brings confusion, distance, and feelings of hopelessness that can feel irresolvable.

This book discussed the consequences and described the steps that those caught up in pornography abuse and addiction can take in order to rebuild healthy lives. It explained the differences between healthy use of pornography and online sexual encounters and its more problematic participants, allowing readers to position themselves and family members along the spectrum from recreation to addiction.

By describing the steps to healing and providing resources for those ready to get help, we wished to offer information and most of all hope to those who have lost parts of their lives and spirit to this problem of isolation and loneliness. Like those who abuse or are addicted to substances, those who find themselves and those they love tangled in the web of pornography problems may feel hopeless and helpless. If you are among them, then you have taken the first step to hope and help by reading this book.

Thousands find help and healing from addictive behaviors by following the kinds of steps outlined here—recognizing their problem, going to a knowledgeable counselor, becoming involved in self-help groups, setting appropriate boundaries, rebuilding their relationships, and restoring balance to their lives. To begin, all that is required is the willingness to get well, be honest, and ask for help.

We wish you all the best in your journey.

NOTES

Chapter 1: Pornography: Fantasy or Obsession?
1. Patrick Carnes, Ph.D., *Don't Call It Love: Recovery from Sexual Addiction* (New York: Bantam Books, 1992; reprint edition); appendix B, pp. 414–417.
2. Pew Charitable Trust, "When Facing a Tough Decision: 60 Million Americans Now Seek the Internet's Help," April 19, 2006, viewable at http://www.pewtrusts.org.
3. Ibid.
4. Family Safe Media, "Pornography Statistics," http://www.familysafemedia.com/pornography_statistics.html.
5. A. Cooper, D. E. Putnam, L. A. Planchon, and S. C. Boies, "Online Sexual Compulsivity: Getting Tangled in the Net," *Sexual Addiction and Compulsivity* 6 (1999): 79–104.
6. A. Cooper, D. L. Delmonico, and R. Burg, "Cybersex Users, Abusers, and Compulsives: New Findings and Implications," *Sexual Addiction and Compulsivity* 7 (2000): 5–29.

Chapter 2: Pleasure Seeker or Porn Addict
7. A. Cooper, D. E. Putnam, L. A. Planchon, and S. C. Boies, "Online Sexual Compulsivity: Getting Tangled in the Net," *Sexual Addiction and Compulsivity* 6 (1999): 79–104; A. Cooper, D. L. Delmonico, and R. Burg, "Cybersex Users, Abusers, and Compulsives: New Findings and Implications," *Sexual Addiction and Compulsivity* 7 (2000): 5–29.
8. Cooper et al., "Cybersex Users," 12.

Chapter 3: Out of Control

9. J. P. Schneider, "Effects of Cybersex Addiction on the Family: Results of a Survey," *Sexual Addiction and Compulsivity* 7 (2000): 31–58.

Chapter 4: The Reality of Romance Online

10. Meghan Daum, "Virtual Love," *The New Yorker*, August 25, 1997.

11. Ellyn Bader and Peter T. Pearson, *In Quest of the Mythical Mate: A Developmental Approach to Diagnosis and Treatment in Couples Therapy* (New York: Brunner/Mazel, 1988)

12. P. Carnes, D. Nonemaker, and N. Skilling, "Gender Differences in Normal and Sexually-Addicted Populations," *American Journal of Preventive Psychiatry and Neurology* 3 (1991): 16–23.

13. Carnes et al., "Gender Differences."

14. Jennifer P. Schneider, "A Qualitative Study of Cybersex Participants: Gender Differences, Recovery Issues, and Implications for Therapists," *Sexual Addiction and Compulsivity* 7 (2000): 249–78.

Chapter 5: The Porn Widow(er)

15. Jennifer Schneider, "Effects of Cybersex Addiction on the Family: Results of a Survey," *Sexual Addiction and Compulsivity* 7 (2000): 31–58.

Chapter 6: Teens, Kids, and Pornography

16. Kimberly J. Mitchell, David Finkelhor, and Janis Wolak, "Risk Factors for and Impact of Online Sexual Solicitation of Youth," *Journal of the American Medical Association* 285 (June 2001): 3011–3014

Chapter 7: Doing the Work to Get Well

17. As encouraged by Patrick Carnes in *Out of the Shadows:*

Understanding Sexual Addiction, (Minneapolis: Compcare
Publications, 1983) and utilized by several of the 12-step
sexual recovery programs,
18. As encouraged by Patrick Carnes in *Out of the Shadows:
Understanding Sexual Addiction*, (Minneapolis: Compcare
Publications, 1983) and utilized by several of the 12-step
sexual recovery programs, p. 42.

Chapter 9: Next Steps: Moving Beyond the Problem
19. Andrea Orr, *Meeting, Mating, (. . . and Cheating): Sex, Love,
and the New World of Online Dating*, (Upper Saddle River,
NJ: Reuters Prentice Hall, 2004).

RESOURCES

Understanding and Recovering from Sex and Pornography Addiction

Augustine Fellowship Staff. *Sex and Love Addicts Anonymous.* Boston: Sex and Love Addicts Anonymous, 1986. The official book of the fellowship of SLAA.

Carnes, Patrick. *Don't Call It Love: Recovery From Sexual Addiction.* New York: Bantam, 1992. Results of research on more than 1,000 sex addicts.

Carnes, Patrick. *Out of the Shadows: Understanding Sexual Addiction.* 3rd ed. Center City, MN: Hazelden Publishing and Educational Services, 2001. The groundbreaking book that explains sex addiction in easily understood terms.

Carnes, Patrick, with Joseph M. Moriarity. *Sexual Anorexia: Overcoming Sexual Self-Hatred.* Center City, MN: Hazelden Publishing and Educational Services, 1997. Explains the flip side of compulsive sexuality: not having sex at all.

Earle, Ralph, and Marcus Earle. *Sex Addiction: Case Studies and Management.* New York: Brunner/Mazel, 1995. Good guide for therapists working with sex addicts.

Hunter, Mic. *Hope and Recovery: A Twelve-Step Guide for Healing from Compulsive Sexual Behavior.* Center City, MN: Hazelden Publishing and Educational Services, 1994. This recovery guide for sex addicts is modeled after the "Big Book" of Alcoholics Anonymous. It explains the problem and provides many people's personal stories.

Kasl, Charlotte Davis. *Women, Sex, and Addiction: A Search for*

Love and Power. New York: Harper, 1990. About women sex addicts and women who hook up with sex addicts.

Maltz, Wendy. *The Sexual Healing Journey: A Guide for Survivors of Sexual Abuse.* Revised ed. New York: Harper-Collins, 2001. Resources to help survivors heal and form healthy relationships to sex.

Weiss, Robert. *Cruise Control: Understanding Sexual Addiction in Gay Men.* Los Angeles: Alyson Books, 2005. The primer for gay men who are sexually addicted. Provides clear, nonjudgmental information for gay men.

For Couples and for Families of Sex Addicts

Beattie, Melody. *Codependent No More: How to Stop Controlling Others and Start Caring for Yourself.* Center City, MN: Hazelden Publishing and Educational Services, 2001.

Carnes, Patrick. *The Betrayal Bond: Breaking Free of Exploitive Relationships.* Deerfield Beach, FL: Health Communications, 1997. This book shows how childhood trauma influences adult relationships.

Corley, M. Deborah and Jennifer P. Schneider. *Disclosing Secrets: What, to Whom, and How Much to Reveal.* Carefree, AZ: Gentle Path Press, 2002. Based on research, this book is a practical guide to making disclosure a positive and constructive experience for couples.

Norwood, Robin. *Women Who Love Too Much: When You Keep Wishing and Hoping He'll Change.* New York: Pocket Books, 1990. The classic book about women who get involved with addicts and how they can heal.

Schaeffer, Brenda. *Is It Love or Is It Addiction?* 2nd ed. Center City, MN: Hazelden Publishing and Educational Services, 1997. Useful for understanding healthy versus unhealthy relationships.

Schneider, Jennifer. *Back from Betrayal: Recovering from His Affairs.* 3rd ed. Tucson, AZ: Recovery Resources Press, 2005. The classic book for women involved with sex-addicted men.

Schneider, Jennifer, and Burt Schneider. *Sex, Lies, and Forgiveness: Couples Speak on Healing from Sex Addiction.,* 3rd ed. Tucson, AZ: Recovery Resources Press, 2004. The classic guide for couples who seek to rebuild their relationship; recently updated.

Spring, Janis Abraham. *After the Affair: Healing the Pain and Rebuilding Trust When a Partner Has Been Unfaithful.* New York: HarperCollins, 1997. No matter what the cause of the affair, this book describes how each party feels and how to recover.

Internet Addiction and Cybersex Addiction

Carnes, Patrick, David Delmonico, Elizabeth Griffin, and Joseph Moriarity. *In the Shadows of the Net: Breaking Free of Compulsive Online Sexual Behavior.* Center City, MN: Hazelden Publishing and Educational Services, 2004.

Cooper, Al, ed. *Cybersex: The Dark Side of the Force.* Philadelphia: Brunner-Routledge, 2000.

Fink, Jeri. *Cyberseduction: Reality in the Age of Psychotechnology.* Amherst, NY: Prometheus Books, 1999. Interesting explanation of why people are so attracted to virtual reality.

Greenfield, David D. *Virtual Addiction: Help for Netheads, Cyber Freaks, and Those Who Love Them* Oakland, CA: New Harbinger Publications, 1999. Written in simple language, a book on how to break addictive connections to the Internet. Some discussion of cybersex addiction.

Tarbox, Katherine. *A Girl's Life Online.* New York: Plume, 2004. A first-person account by a young teen who inadvertently became involved online with a pedophile.

Young, Kimberly S. *Caught in the Net: How to Recognize the Signs of Internet Addiction—And a Winning Strategy for Recovery.* New York: John Wiley & Sons, 1998. The consequences of excessive involvement with Internet activities but not cybersex.

Online Resources for Parents and Teens

Below is a list of online resources for sex education and for Internet safety for teens. Some of the sites are intended for parents, others for teens. It's advisable for parents to check out all these Web sites and recommend the teen-friendly ones to their children. A good start would be to read the article, "Teen Safety on the Information Highway" by Larry Magid at www.safeteens.com/safeteens.htm

INTERNET BEHAVIOR CONSULTING
www.internetbehavior.com
In addition to helpful information online, this company has professionals available for consultation, training and intervention for problematic online behavior. Their online newsletter *Cyber Times* is informative.

GETNETWISE.ORG
www.getnetwise.org
Helpful site for keeping children safe online, stopping unwanted e-mail and spam, protecting your computer from hackers and viruses, and keeping your personal information private.

Enough Is Enough
www.protectkids.com

Kid-friendly site with information on Internet dangers, the
harmful effects of pornography, and child sexual abuse;
resources; youth safety rules, parents' rules and tools, safety
tools; and links for reporting cybercrime.

ADVOCATES FOR YOUTH
www.advocatesforyouth.org
"Helping young people make informed decisions about sex."

COALITION FOR POSITIVE SEXUALITY
www.positive.org
Kid-friendly site to educate teens on healthy sexuality.

SEXUALITY INFORMATION AND EDUCATION COUNCIL
    OF THE UNITED STATES
www.siecus.com
Much information on sexuality.

SAFEKIDS.COM
www.safekids.com
Kid-friendly site for safe Internet and technology use.

WEB WISE KIDS
www.webwisekids.com
Helps to prepare children, teens, and adults to make wise
choices when using the Internet.

I-SAFE AMERICA, INC.
www.isafe.org
Internet safety education resources

CYBERSMART! EDUCATION COMPANY
www.cybersmart.org
Kid-friendly educational site on internet safety

NATIONAL COALITION FOR THE PROTECTION OF
    CHILDREN AND FAMILIES
www.filterreview.com
Information to help you select the right ISP and filtering/
    blocking or monitoring systems.

WIREDKIDS, INC.
www.wiredkids.org
Internet safety, safe sites, and products.

Twelve-Step Sexual Recovery Meeting Information

The following list briefly describes recovery programs for sex and porn addiction, their focus, and attendance. Contact the national offices by phone or visit their Web sites for more specific meeting information, location, and times. All these groups are self-help programs for people who wish to recover from any type of compulsive sexual behavior. Web sites for each fellowship are also listed below.

Each Web site offers information primarily as outreach to new and current members, providing information, support services, and links to related organizations. The Web sites can be viewed from all current browsers. They all appear easy to understand and are user-friendly. Several of the sites have online meetings, a feature of particular value to those either geographically or physically unable to attend actual support meetings. These online meetings are hosted and managed by the particular support group; therefore the content of the discussions is maintained within appropriate boundaries. Please be advised that Web site addresses frequently change and an internet search engine may be needed to find the recommended site.

Addict and Offender Groups

SEXAHOLICS ANONYMOUS (SA)

A national 12-step program, employing the most restrictive definition of sexual sobriety: "No sexual behavior outside of a marital relationship." The membership of this group is primarily heterosexual men, but an increasing number of women attend. SA has an affiliated program for spouses and families of sex addicts and offenders called S-Anon. Heterosexual men who are in a committed, married relationship would benefit most from the recovery materials available from this fellowship. The sex offender population is also more heavily represented in SA for this same reason. Those with more conservative religious beliefs often find themselves more comfortable here. Some people consider SA to be less supportive of sexual orientations other than heterosexual, although this varies from meeting to meeting. Newcomers and old-timers alike, as well as people who speak Spanish or German, can find resources. SA is also the only 12-step group that offers a program for prisoners. Spouses will find links for family members on SA's web site.

Web site: www.sa.org

E-mail: saico@sa.org

Phone: (866) 424-8777; (615) 370-6062

SEXUAL ADDICTS ANONYMOUS (SAA)

A national 12-step program that encourages participants to define their sexual sobriety by working with other recovering members. Attendance is mixed, primarily men of any sexual orientation with some limited female attendance. SAA attracts the largest and broadest base of all of the 12-step sexual addiction recovery programs. SAA has an affiliated program for partners of sexual addicts called COSA (Codependents of Sex Addicts).

Web site: www.sexaa.org:

E-mail: info@saa-recovery.org
Phone: (800) 477-8191; (713) 869-4902

SEXUAL COMPULSIVES ANONYMOUS (SCA)
A 12-step program found in most major urban areas.
   Membership is primarily, but not exclusively, gay and
   bisexual men and some women. Participants define their
   sexual sobriety through the boundaries of a written plan
   that evolves through working with other recovering
   members. SCA has no formal partners program. People
   with differing sexual orientations would find this program
   most beneficial.
Web site: www.sca-recovery.org
E-mail: info@SCArecovery.org
Phone: (800) 977-HEAL; (212) 606-3778

SEX AND LOVE ADDICTS ANONYMOUS (S.L.A.A.)
This 12-step program focuses on addictive sexual and
   romantic relationships. S.L.A.A. is helpful for sexual
   addicts as well as people who consistently involve
   themselves in abusive, nonnurturing relationships. This
   program attracts both men and women. S.L.A.A. is the
   most broadly supportive of women of all the 12-step
   sexual addictions organizations. What differentiates this
   group is that it has a focus on the recovery from problems
   related to romantic dependency, romantic relationships,
   emotional dependency, and social or emotional anorexia.
Web site: www.slaafws.org
E-mail: info@slaafws.org
Phone: (210) 828-7900

SEXUAL RECOVERY ANONYMOUS (SRA)
This is a "non-higher power" 12-step program for sex addicts
   and sex offenders modeled after Rational Recovery, which

focuses on spirituality and self-love rather than the notion of a "higher power." SRA meetings are limited in number and in scope, with scattered meetings in the New York, Connecticut, New Jersey tristate area, as well as in Los Angeles, Atlanta, and Vancouver, BC, Canada. However, SRA is open to all those who seek healing and recovery.
Web site: www.sexualrecovery.org
E-mail: info@sexualrecovery.org

Partner and Couple Groups

S-ANON
A national 12-step program for partners and families of sex addicts and sex offenders. Although primarily married women attend, there are also many single members. The fellowship welcomes anyone whose life has been affected in the present or past by relationship with a sex addict. S-Anon is affiliated with SA and supports S-Ateen, a program for children of sex addicts.
Web site: www.sanon.org
E-mail: sanon@sanon.org
Phone: (800) 210-8141; (615) 833-3152

CODEPENDENTS OF SEX ADDICTS (COSA)
A national 12-step program for partners of sex addicts and sex offenders. The fellowship is affiliated with SAA. Anyone who is in relationship with a sexual addict is welcome. Because of the links available to the family groups, this Web site makes it easy for spouses and other family members to find appropriate groups for their recovery. One option made available through this organization is online meetings. Information describing what an online meeting is, how to join one, a listing of current online meetings, and how to start an online meeting, is clearly laid out.

Web site: www.cosa-recovery.org
E-mail: info@cosa-recovery.org
Phone: (763) 537-6904

RECOVERING COUPLES ANONYMOUS (RCA)
A 12-step program that helps both addicts and their partners
work on issues of commitment, intimacy and mutual
recovery. All couple—married and nonmarried, gay and
straight—are welcome. The fellowship is open to couples
dealing with any addiction, but at least 50 percent of
members have a sexual addiction problem.
Web site: www.recovering-couples.org
E-mail: rca_email@recovering-couples.org
Phone: (510) 663-2312

FAITH-BASED RESOURCES
Books

Arterburn, Stephen and Fred Stoeker with Mike Yorkey. *Every
Man's Battle: Winning the War on Sexual Temptation.*
Colorado Springs: WaterBrook Press, 2000.
Earle, Ralph and Mark Laaser. *The Pornography Trap: Setting
Pastors and Laypersons Free from Sexual Addiction.* Kansas
City, MO: Beacon Hill Press, 2002.
Laaser, Mark. *L.I.F.E Guide for Men.* Longwood, FL: Xulon
Press, 2002.
Means, Marsha. *Living with Your Husband's Secret Wars.*
Grand Rapids, MI: Revell, 1999.
Schaumburg, Harry W. *False Intimacy: Understanding the
Struggle of Sexual Addiction.* Colorado Springs, CO:
NavPress, 1997.
Wilson, Kathryn and Wilson, Paul. *Stone Cold in a Warm
Bed: One Couple's Battle with Pornography.* Bountiful, UT:
Horizon Books, 1998.

Organizations and Websites

FAITHFUL AND TRUE MINISTRIES
Faith-based clinical intensives for men, women, spouses, and
   couples.
2312 Peachford Rd., Suite C
Atlanta, GA 30338
Web site: www.faithfulandtruemarriages.com
Phone: (770) 457-3028

L.I.F.E. MINISTRIES INTERNATIONAL
More than 125 support groups in the United States, and some
   outside. They have a telephone support group for those
   who have no access to local groups. The contact Web site
   for the telephone group is: www.telelifegroups.org
P.O. Box 952317
Lake Mary, FL 32795
Web site: www.freedomeveryday.org
E-mail: info@freedomeveryday.org
Phone: (866) 408-LIFE

FIRES OF DARKNESS MINISTRIES
Their mission is "reaching out to porn addicts and the people
   who love them."
P.O. Box 211
Madison, TN 37116
Web site: www.firesofdarkness.com
E-mail: counseling@firesofdarkness.com

NEW LIFE MINISTRIES
They consider themselves to be "America's largest faith-based
   broadcasting and counseling organization."
P.O. Box 1018
Laguna Beach, CA 92652

Web site: www.newlife.com
Phone: (800) NEW-LIFE (639-5433)

Additional Organizations and Web Sites

THE SOCIETY OF ADVANCEMENT OF SEXUAL HEALTH (SASH)

This is a private nonprofit organization dedicated to the
promotion of public and professional recognition,
awareness, and understanding of sexual addiction, sexual
compulsivity, and sexual offending. SASH is an educational
and referral resource for sex and porn addicts, sexual
offenders, and any counseling, criminal justice, or research
professional in need of information or referrals, and for
the media. The Web site of SASH contains articles, position
papers, national referral information for therapists, and
information on treatment centers, as well as material about
their annual national conference.

SASH
P.O. Box 725544
Atlanta, GA 31139
Web site: www.sash.net
E-mail: sash@sash.net

CYBERSEXUALADDICTION.COM

An informational Web site about cyberporn and cybersex
addiction problems with helpful links and information.
Web site: www.cybersexualaddiction.com

THE HEALTHY MIND

Clinical psychologist David Bissette, PsyD, from Washington,
DC, offers a wealth of information about pornography,
sexual addiction, and recovery. Pages include explanations

about the nature of addiction and helpful worksheets for establishing and maintaining sobriety.
Web site: www.healthymind.com
Phone: (703) 705-6161

JENNIFER P. SCHNEIDER
The Web site for author Jennifer P. Schneider. Provides the full text of research articles on sex addiction and its effects on the family, and information about her other books about sex addiction and family recovery.
1500 North Wilmot Road, Suite B-250
Tucson, AZ 85712
Web site: www.jenniferschneider.com
E-mail: jennifer@jenniferschneider.com
Phone: (520) 721-7886

SEXHELP.COM
International sex addiction expert Patrick Carnes, PhD, offers addiction and recovery resources. It features the leading books, videos, and audios in the field of sex addiction and recovery.
Web site: www.SexHelp.com

THE SEXUAL RECOVERY INSTITUTE
Web site for the assessment and treatment program of author Robert Weiss, MSW, LCSW, CAS, clinical director. Provides extensive articles and self-test, helpful links, and information about treatment.
822 S. Robertson Blvd, Suite #303
Los Angeles, CA 90035
Web site: www.sexualrecovery.com
E-mail: info@sexualrecovery.com
Phone: (310) 360-0130

ABOUT THE AUTHORS

ROBERT WEISS, L.C.S.W., C.A.S. is founder and executive director of The Sexual Recovery Institute, an outpatient sexual addiction treatment center based in Los Angeles. An acknowledged professional in the assessment and treatment of persons with addictive sexual disorders and sexual offending, he is coauthor with Dr. Jennifer Schneider of *Untangling the Web: Sex, Porn and Fantasy Obsession in the Internet Age,* second edition (originally titled *Cybersex Exposed*); author of *Cruise Control: Understanding Sex Addiction in Gay Men*; and author of "Treating Sexual Addiction" in *The Handbook of Addictive Disorders*. Currently Weiss serves on the editorial board of *The Journal of Sexual Addiction and Compulsivity*.

A graduate of University of California, Los Angeles, with a master's degree in social work, he was trained under the direction of Dr. Patrick Carnes. Weiss is a former board member and committee chair of the National Council on Sexual Addiction and Compulsivity (now the Society for the Advancement of Sexual Health) and has presented for The UCLA Neuro-Psychiatric Institute, the American Association of Sexuality Educators, Counselors, and Therapists, the National Association of Social Workers, and in Washington, D.C., at the National Institutes of Health, among many others. He provides clinical training for numerous multi-addiction treatment centers, including The Gentle Path Program, Sierra Tucson, The Life Healing Center, and The Meadows. He has appeared on *The Oprah Winfrey Show, The Today Show, Dateline*

NBC, CNN, *20/20,* HBO, and *ABC World News Tonight.*

He lives in Los Angeles.

JENNIFER SCHNEIDER, M.D., PH.D, is a physician in Tucson, Arizona, specializing in addiction medicine and pain management. For nearly twenty years she has been a researcher, speaker, and author in the field of sex addiction, with a particular interest in the effects of sex addiction on the family and in sexual exploitation by professionals.

Dr. Schneider is the author of *Back from Betrayal: Recovering from His Affairs; Sex, Lies, and Forgiveness: Couples Speak on Healing From Sex Addiction; The Wounded Healer: Addiction-Sensitive Therapy for the Sexually Exploitative Professional* (with Dr. Richard Irons); *Disclosing Secrets: When, to Whom, and How Much to Reveal* (with Dr. Deborah Corley); *Embracing Recovery from Chemical Dependency* (with Dr. Deborah Corley and Dr. Richard Irons); *Living with Chronic Pain*; and *Untangling the Web: Sex, Porn, and Fantasy Obsession in the Internet Age,* second edition (with Robert Weiss; originally titled *Cybersex Exposed*). She has also authored numerous book chapters and scholarly papers on various aspects of sex addiction.

Dr. Schneider is a former board member of the National Council on Sexual Addiction and Compulsivity (now the Society for the Advancement of Sexual Health), and the 1998 winner of NCSAC's Patrick Carnes Award for lifetime contributions to the field of sex addiction. In 1999, 2000, and 2003 she won NCSAC's Readers' Choice Award for the best article in the society's journal, *Sexual Addiction and Compulsivity: The Journal of Treatment and Prevention.*

For many years she has been associate editor of *Sexual Addiction and Compulsivity.* A frequent lecturer to both professionals and lay people, she has appeared as an expert on numerous national radio and television shows in the United States and Canada, including *The Oprah Winfrey Show.*

INDEX

D

E